COYOTE'S PANTRY

COYOTE'S PANTRY

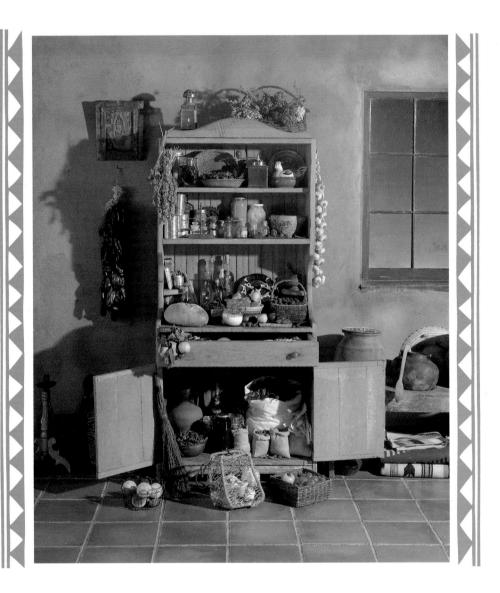

Southwest Seasonings and at Home Flavoring Techniques

MARK MILLER and MARK KIFFIN

with John Harrisson

Recipes from Santa Fe's Famous Coyote Cafe

TEN SPEED PRESS

To Bill and Marilyn, Diane and Melissa. Thanks for all your love and support.

With apologies to General Patton, a spicy, tasty recipe violently executed today is far better than a perfect, bland recipe executed next week.

Cover and book design by Fifth Street Design, Berkeley CA.

Photography by Valerie Santagto.

Additional photography by Brenton Beck, Pedro J. Gonzalez and Bill Schwob.

Photo styling by Paulette Tavormina.

Claiborne Gallery provided trasteros, glassware, and artifacts. Thanks to Omer Claiborne for his generosity, and to Caroline Adams for her assistance.

Cover tinwork by Kyle Streck, Streck Family

Porcelain ceramics on page 92 by Heidi Loewen.

Table surfaces by El Paso Import Company.

Spanish Pueblo Doors (Designer: Will Ott) provided surfaces for photography.

Coyote logo by Harry Fonseca.

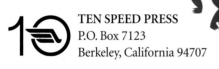

TEN SPEED PRESS
P.O. Box 7123
Berkeley, California 94707

Library of Congress Cataloging-in-Publication Data

Miller, Mark Charles, 1949-
Coyote's pantry: southwest seasonings and at-home flavoring techniques / by Mark Miller & Mark Kiffin.
p. cm.
Includes index.
ISBN 0-89815-494-4 1. Coyote Cafe (Santa Fe, N.M.) 2. Condiments.
3. Sauces. 4. Marinades. 5. Cookery, American—Southwestern style.
I. Kiffin, Mark. II. Title.
TX819.A1M55 1993
641.6'382—dc2092-24211

Printed in Korea

2 3 4 5 - 97 96 95 94 93

We wish to thank:

Cindi Jeakle for putting up with the long hours and for being there in spirit;

Trez Noone Harrisson, likewise;

Tommy Birdwell and Mark Arnao for their recipe-testing expertise and patience;

Karl Schwirian for facilitating things in the kitchen;

The Alvarez brothers and "all the boys in the back" for their assistance;

Dave Hoemann, Brett Kemmerer, and Greg O'Byrne—Coyote's management team—for their support and encouragement;

The rest of the Coyote staff for their help in the creative process;

Coyote Cafe's customers, for appreciating and requesting so many of these recipes;

Elizabeth Berry and the other first-class purveyors, without whom life would be difficult;

Ric Nardin: now we can exchange books!

Jackie Wan, for her suggestions and editorial panache;

And last but not least, Marie Smith, Phil Wood, George Young, JoAnn Deck, and all the other folks at Ten Speed Press without whom this book would merely be so much computer disk-space.

TABLE OF CONTENTS

COYOTE'S
PANTRY

INTRODUCTION

One of my fondest childhood memories is of my grandmother's pantry. It was a cool, secret place where all kinds of goodies were stored—pies and baked goods, jams, honey, rich butter, bottled fruit, tea, coffee, chocolates, beans, and such exotic ingredients as olives and capers. Occasionally, a ham would appear in the pantry, and there it would sit in the days before plastic wrap, aluminum foil, or refrigeration. Marvelous aromas drifted out of her pantry, all beckoning to me. I recall the smell of hot breads left there to cool after coming out of the oven, and the scent of sweet spices such as nutmeg or cinnamon, which would fill my mind with images of delicious pies.

Since the pantry was officially off-limits to me (I was a small boy who would happily get sick from "sampling" all the different great-tasting food there), I was all the more intrigued and curious about this wonderful place, drawn as if by a magnet. Many of the shelves and tall cabinets were out of reach, and I became consumed with the desire to somehow get into those cupboards. This was a case where out-of-reach was definitely not out-of-mind.

Though I couldn't have expressed it at the time, I know that there was much more to my grandmother's pantry than delicious homemade foods and the element of mystery. A more important factor, and one that I can appreciate now, was what her pantry symbolized to me—the strength of our family ties and traditions, nurturance, caring, safety.

I now discover that the magical delights of the pantry are something in which most of us have shared. It seems to me that the current interest in home cooking reflects the American culinary continuum, and is directly related to those formative experiences from our collective pasts. In the age of the microwave oven and fast-food chains, we have come full circle, to the point where quality and taste are considered as important as are convenience and speed, and a premium is placed on wholesome, carefully prepared, homemade foods.

Of course cooking from scratch takes time and energy, but the rewards make it worthwhile. Homemade foods taste better than mass-market convenience foods because you can select the highest quality ingredients. They are more healthful because you can eliminate additives and preservatives, and control the amount of fat and salt used. In general, homemade foods are less expensive then their commercially made counterparts. Finally, there are the intangible benefits that come from making your own foods: the sense of accomplishment, the flexibility in creating flavorings to suit your own palate, and the opportunity to express yourself creatively and to connect with the traditions of by-gone generations.

Before the advent of refrigeration, preserving foods and putting foods by for the future were a matter of survival (except for those few peoples who lived in climates where nature provided a plentiful supply year-round). The earliest European settlers in North America were keenly aware of the need to stock preserved fruits, vegetables, meats, and staples to get them through the harsh winters. Much of this they learned how to do from the Native Americans, whose custom it was to dry beans, corn, squash, chiles, and meats for storage.

Refrigeration and speedy transportation have made it unnecessary to stockpile enough food each year to make it through the winter or as a hedge against a season of poor crops. Most of us can go down to the local supermarket and pick up whatever we want whenever we need it. There's no need to put up 100 jars of apples or tomatoes, store sacks of beans or rice, or cure sides of bacon, and we don't have to wait six months or a year for a shipment of spices from the orient.

Still, I think we all take comfort in a well-stocked pantry. Even in new houses being built today, pantries are making a come-back; and this is a welcome culinary connection to a time-honored tradition of setting aside a place for keeping special foods. Setting up and maintaining a pantry is easier today than ever before. Specialty and ethnic markets carry a wide range of exotic ingredients, and what you can't find there, you can mail-order. If you consider the refrigerator and freezer as an extension of the pantry, the possibilities are limitless.

Over recent years, we have witnessed an explosion of interest in new ingredients and innovative dishes. Eating habits have changed: we have become more adventurous, and at the same time, more critical, demanding that our food be both flavorful and healthful. Southwestern cuisine, in particular, fits right into these changing patterns: the food is robust, yet relatively low in cholesterol and fat. For instance, instead of rich sauces made with butter and cream, you will find sauces and salsas based on vegetables and fruit. (You will also find chiles, from mild to torrid, used in almost everything!)

This book is aimed at providing the home cook with an understanding of Southwestern flavorings and seasonings and preparation techniques. It will explain how to set up a Southwestern pantry, and how to draw upon it to create Southwestern-style condiments, sauces, and other accompaniments that will make your cooking come alive with taste and expression. At the same time, it will explore the history and background of the various dishes. One of my fascinations with Southwestern cuisine is that it represents a living tradition, incorporating many different cultural influences, including Native American, Mexican, Hispanic, and European. It epitomizes the growing interest in ethnicity in the American diet, and the more adventurous approach that this implies.

✤ *Setting Up the Southwestern Pantry* ✤

You don't need to be wearing cowboy boots to get your Southwestern pantry in gear. It's really just a state of mind. The pantry I keep now is not so far removed from the pantry that captivated me as a child. I might use a *trastero*, a traditional Southwestern cupboard, like those pictured in this book, and in it you'd find some items my grandmother never heard of—dried habanero chiles, tamarind paste, tequila. But the spirit and concept are the same, and the tradition goes on unbroken.

Many of the basic ingredients in the Southwestern pantry are the same essentials to be found in any kitchen anywhere, and can be purchased at your local supermarket. Others are more regional in availability, but even so, due to the growth in popularity of Southwestern cuisine, most can be found locally wherever you live. In the event you have difficulty obtaining any ingredients, you can refer to the Source List on page 123.

The list that follows refers only to items that can be stored in the pantry for weeks or months, so most fresh produce such as chiles, tomatoes, tomatillos, and fresh herbs are not included. However, fresh produce with a longer shelf-life, such as onions, garlic, ginger, and citrus fruit, are included here, as well as a few dairy products. Italicized items are those that you will probably use less frequently; alter the lists to suit your own style of cooking.

OILS AND VINEGARS

- [ ] virgin olive oil
- [ ] extra-virgin olive oil
- [ ] vegetable oil (corn or canola oil)
- [ ] peanut oil
- [ ] unseasoned rice vinegar
- [ ] red wine vinegar
- [ ] white wine vinegar
- [ ] cider vinegar
- [ ] Italian balsamic vinegar
- [ ] sherry vinegar (preferably Spanish)
- [ ] *lard*
- [ ] *grapeseed oil*
- [ ] *sunflower seed oil*
- [ ] *sesame oil*
- [ ] *champagne vinegar*

HERBS AND SPICES

- [ ] dried oregano
- [ ] dried sage
- [ ] dried thyme
- [ ] dried bay leaves
- [ ] dried rosemary
- [ ] cumin seeds
- [ ] allspice berries
- [ ] cinnamon sticks
- [ ] canela sticks
- [ ] whole cloves
- [ ] peppercorns
- [ ] nutmeg
- [ ] *Mexican asafran, or saffron threads*
- [ ] *lampong and/or tellicherry pepper*
- [ ] *achiote seeds*
- [ ] *gumbo filé*
- [ ] *dried juniper berries*
- [ ] *caraway seeds*
- [ ] *mustard seeds*
- [ ] *coriander seeds*
- [ ] *celery seeds*

CHILES AND CHILE PRODUCTS

- [ ] dried New Mexico red chiles
- [ ] dried ancho chiles
- [ ] dried chiles de árbol
- [ ] chipotle chiles (dried and canned *en adobo*)
- [ ] pure red chile powder (such as chile molido)
- [ ] cayenne chile powder
- [ ] chile caribe (red chile flakes, with seeds)
- [ ] *dried habanero chiles*
- [ ] *dried mulato chiles*
- [ ] *dried chiles negro (pasilla chiles)*
- [ ] *frozen green chiles*
- [ ] *chile pasado*

SAUCES AND CONDIMENTS

- [ ] Tabasco sauce
- [ ] Worcestershire sauce
- [ ] soy sauce
- [ ] ketchup
- [ ] mayonnaise
- [ ] Dijon mustard
- [ ] whole-grain mustard
- [ ] dried mustard powder

SWEETENERS

- [ ] granulated sugar
- [ ] brown sugar
- [ ] honey
- [ ] *dark molasses*
- [ ] *cane sugar*
- [ ] *maple syrup*
- [ ] *maple sugar*
- [ ] *Mexican piloncillo sugar*

PRODUCE

- [ ] onions (yellow, red, and white)
- [ ] shallots
- [ ] potatoes
- [ ] carrots
- [ ] garlic
- [ ] horseradish root
- [ ] ginger
- [ ] lemons
- [ ] limes
- [ ] oranges
- [ ] grapefruits

BEANS, RICE, PASTA

- [ ] dried black beans
- [ ] dried pinto beans
- [ ] dried white beans
- [ ] dried flageolet beans
- [ ] Texmati or long-grain rice
- [ ] assorted pastas
- [ ] tortillas (corn and flour)
- [ ] *wild rice*
- [ ] *arborio rice*
- [ ] *couscous*

FLOUR

- [ ] all-purpose flour
- [ ] masa harina
- [ ] cornmeal
- [ ] bread crumbs

NUTS AND SEEDS

- [ ] pecans
- [ ] pine nuts (piñons)
- [ ] walnuts
- [ ] peanuts
- [ ] *almonds*
- [ ] *pumpkin seeds*
- [ ] *sesame seeds*

MISCELLANEOUS

- [ ] chicken stock (preferably homemade)
- [ ] vegetable stock (preferably homemade)
- [ ] tomato purée
- [ ] canned anchovies
- [ ] bacon
- [ ] beer (light and dark)
- [ ] white wine
- [ ] red wine
- [ ] sherry (dry)
- [ ] tequila
- [ ] *capers*
- [ ] *prickly pear syrup*
- [ ] *tamarind paste*
- [ ] *beef jerky*
- [ ] *unsweetened chocolate*
- [ ] *Ibarra (Mexican) chocolate*
- [ ] *bourbon*
- [ ] *gin*
- [ ] *dark rum*
- [ ] *Marsala or Madeira*
- [ ] *muscat wine*

DRIED FRUITS AND VEGETABLES

- [ ] raisins
- [ ] currants
- [ ] sun-dried tomatoes (dehydrated and/or packed in olive oil)
- [ ] *dried cherries*
- [ ] *dried apricots (unsulphured)*
- [ ] *dried wild mushrooms*

DAIRY PRODUCTS

- [ ] unsalted butter
- [ ] goat cheese
- [ ] Parmesan cheese (and/or Asiago cheese)
- [ ] eggs (preferably free-range)

❖ *Basic Rules of Southwestern Cooking* ❖

There's more than one way to skin a cat, as they say, and we're sure that applies to Southwestern cooking as well. We don't believe in strict procedures or set ways of doing things, and we encourage you to experiment with recipes and ingredients. But there are a few things we absolutely insist upon!

- *Rule 1*. Always use produce and ingredients that are as fresh as possible. Buy ripe, unblemished fruit and vegetables, and good-quality oil, vinegar, spices, etc. If in doubt, discard questionable ingredients, as one bad apple can spoil the barrel (as they also say). It's a waste of your valuable time to use mediocre ingredients, and always remember that the food you make will only be as good as the components you use, however dazzling the recipe.

- *Rule 2*. For most of these recipes, it's best to use nonreactive mixing bowls, pans, and utensils (stainless steel, glass, enamel, porcelain, etc.), especially when the recipe calls for acidic ingredients such as vinegar or fruit juice.

- *Rule 3*. In general, pantry items are best kept out of direct sunlight and away from heat. They should be stored in a cool, dry place, well away from any dampness.

- *Rule 4*. If you aren't a skilled cook or if you don't feel particularly at ease in the kitchen, start with the simpler recipes and work up to the more involved ones.

- *Rule 5*. It's better to make a small amount and finish it up before it spoils than to be overly ambitious and make too much. Cut recipes in half if necessary.

- *Rule 6*. It's best to prepare foods when you have enough time and when you can enjoy and savor the accomplishment and challenge of doing it yourself.

SALSAS AND CHIPS

Whether in the sense of food or in the context of music and dance, the word *salsa* means excitement, action, vibrant colors, and, above all, fun. From Mexican street stands to Southwestern restaurants to taquerias everywhere, salsas with their mini-fiestas of colors, flavors, and textures have always provided a feast for both the eye and the palate. More recently, salsas have been popping up on menus all across the United States, everywhere from roadhouse diners to four-star restaurants. And now we invite you to join in on the fun by making your own salsas to serve at home.

You don't need fancy, exotic, gourmet ingredients to compose a salsa. All you need are fresh fruits or vegetables as a base, an intensely flavored seasoning such as chiles, citrus juice, or vinegar to give it a lively tang, and some flavorful herbs, such as cilantro, basil, marjoram, or mint, or aromatic spices, such as cumin or cinnamon, to give more character.

In general, salsas are easy and quick to prepare, and making them doesn't involve complicated techniques or expensive equipment. Usually just a knife and cutting board will do, and sometimes a blender or food processor. Best of all, salsas are natural and healthful: since cooking is rarely involved, their nutritional value is not diminished.

In preparing salsas, the most important thing to bear in mind (unless you are using a blender or food processor) is that the ingredients should be cut as carefully as possible into uniform dice or shapes in order to make their appearance as attractive as possible. This also ensures that the texture of the salsa will be crunchy rather than mushy. The smaller the dice, the more flavors that are in each forkful, and the more balanced and complex the harmony of the salsa becomes.

People usually think of salsas just as an accompaniment for chips, but they are multidimensional and have infinite applications. You can make salsas to go with anything from eggs to enchiladas, from filet mignon to (yes) chips, and alter them to suit your personal preferences (you can make them mild, medium, or picante, smooth or chunky, thick or thin). Using salsas allows you to be creative and to personalize your cooking.

Salsas are found virtually all over the world – their equivalents are found in the cuisines of Asia, Africa, southern Europe, Central and South America, and Mexico, too, of course. And now you can join the parade. Get into the habit of preparing salsas regularly and make every day a salsa day. Start with whatever vegetables or fruits are in season, use the recipes here as a guide, and then experiment with your own combinations. Remember, about the only thing salsas don't go with are hot fudge sundaes!

SALSA FRESCA

When you think of salsas, you probably think first of salsa fresca – *the typical tomato-chile-onion salsa served with chips when you sit down in some Southwestern, Tex-Mex, and Mexican restaurants. It's a shame that* salsa fresca *is usually only seen in this context, as it can be used in many ways and makes a great seasoning or an additional side dish for a meal. Salsa fresca is used in Mexico the same way that ketchup is used in the United States, to add a little verve to plain foods. But* salsa fresca *is better than ketchup because it is made fresh. A proper* salsa fresca *contains ripe red tomatoes, a hint of crunchy onion, the bite of green chile, the tang of fresh lime, and the refreshing aroma of cilantro. The addition of a little beer (a northern Mexican tradition) helps bring out an authentic flavor. It seems appropriate that the colors of this salsa (red, white, and green) are the same as those in the Mexican flag.*

2 tablespoons peeled white onion, cut into ⅛-inch dice
8 plum tomatoes (about 1 pound), cut into ¼-inch dice
2 serrano chiles, cut into ⅛-inch dice, with seeds
2 tablespoons finely chopped fresh cilantro leaves
1 teaspoon sugar or more, to taste
¼ cup Mexican beer, such as Dos Equis
1 teaspoon salt
1 tablespoon fresh lime juice

Place the onion in a strainer, rinse with hot water, and drain. Combine all the ingredients in a mixing bowl and mix well. Add a little more sugar if the tomatoes are acidic, but make sure the salsa does not taste of sugar. Chill in the refrigerator for at least 30 minutes before serving to allow the flavors to combine.

Serving suggestions: Serve chilled with grilled meats or fish, tacos, enchiladas, beans, and with corn chips. This salsa makes cooked foods come alive with freshness.

Storage: Best used the same day or the tomatoes become watery. If keeping longer, add a little vinegar or more lime juice to help preserve the flavor.

Preparation time: About 20 minutes

Yield: About 2 cups

TOMATILLO-SERRANO SALSA

Tomatillos (also called jitomates *in Mexico) are indigenous to the New World. They look very much like small green tomatoes, and have a crisp, refreshing, tart flavor with tones of rhubarb, plum, lemon, and apple. They are available in Hispanic and specialty produce markets year-round. Look for tomatillos that are firm and dark green in color – do not buy soft or yellow tomatillos. Small tomatillos are best as they have smaller seeds; tomatillos store well in the refrigerator. Remove the paper husk and rinse them well before use as they have a sticky surface. This salsa is a good alternative to* Salsa Fresca *(see preceding recipe), especially when good fresh tomatoes are unavailable, and it is just as easy to make. It always arouses great interest whenever we prepare it at cooking demonstrations and book signings.*

15 tomatillos, husked, rinsed, and roughly chopped
3 serrano chiles with seeds, roughly chopped
1 teaspoon sugar
½ cup chopped fresh cilantro leaves
1¾ teaspoons salt
1 cup water
2 tablespoons fresh lime juice
1 ripe avocado, peeled, pitted, and roughly chopped

Pulse the tomatillos, serranos, sugar, cilantro, salt, and ½ cup water in a blender until smooth. Add the lime juice, avocado, and the remaining ½ cup water and pulse again until the salsa is smooth and even-colored, but not puréed.

Serving suggestions: This classic *salsa verde* (green salsa) is an excellent all-purpose salsa. Serve it cold or at room temperature with tapas or hors d'oeuvres, fish tacos, quesadillas, smoked salmon, grilled fish such as halibut and sea bass, and most seafood. It can also be served cold as a shrimp cocktail sauce.

Storage: Can be stored in the refrigerator up to 2 days, but the longer it is held, the more it loses its bright green color.

Preparation time: About 30 minutes

Yield: About 3 cups

GREEN CHILE SALSA

People sometimes ask me about the two different varieties of New Mexico chile, the red and the green. They are always surprised to learn that the two are actually the same chile. The green are simply harvested before they turn red. The chile harvest in New Mexico begins in late August and continues until the end of September or the beginning of October. A good deal of the crop is harvested green, and roasted and then frozen to preserve it for the winter months. The remainder is picked when fully ripened and red, then dried and used to make red chile sauces and chile powders. New Mexico green chiles can vary greatly in heat from mild to scorching, so it is worth tasting one before you start cooking to determine its degree of spiciness.

In Mexico, salsa verde is usually made with a combination of tomatillos and chiles (see the preceding recipe): this one is made with green chiles, and makes a great alternative. A good rule of thumb is that green chiles go with anything, and make everything taste better!

Note: If fresh New Mexico green chiles are not available, use 8 Anaheim chiles plus 2 serrano chiles with seeds to adjust for spiciness. Frozen New Mexico chiles can also be substituted. Most frozen chiles are labeled either mild, medium, hot, or extra hot.

2 tablespoons virgin olive oil
1/2 onion, peeled and cut into 1/4-inch dice
I clove roasted garlic, peeled and finely minced
8 New Mexico green chiles, roasted, peeled, and
    seeded, cut into 1/4-inch dice (about I cup)
1/2 teaspoon cumin seeds, toasted and finely ground
1/2 teaspoon dried oregano, toasted and finely ground
2 cups water
I teaspoon minced fresh cilantro leaves
3/4 teaspoon salt

Heat the oil in a saucepan over medium heat. Add the onion and garlic and sauté until softened, about 5 minutes. Add the chiles, cumin, and oregano, and mix thoroughly. Add the water and bring to a boil. Reduce heat and simmer slowly for 20 minutes; add more water if the salsa is too thick. Remove from heat and when cool, stir in the cilantro and season with salt.

Serving suggestions: This is a perfect salsa verde or green salsa: serve it chilled with tortilla chips, quesadillas, enchiladas, meats, seafood, and fish.

Storage: Keeps for 2 to 3 days in the refrigerator.

Variation: Fold in some diced, cooked vegetables such as oven-roasted tomatoes, grilled eggplant, and squash.

Preparation time: About 45 minutes

Yield: About 1½ cups

HATCH CHILE SALSA

The area around Hatch in southern New Mexico is the most famous chile growing area in the United States – the town even holds a chile festival every year on Labor Day weekend. In the fall, along roadsides and outside supermarkets, green chiles are roasted by the bushel in large gas-fired metal cages, exuding a heady, spicy aroma into the crisp, cool air. At this time of year you can see people wheeling home cartloads of freshly roasted chiles to put up for the long winter months.

Note: This salsa will taste best if you can get fresh New Mexico green chiles, especially if they come from the Hatch area. If they're not available, use 8 Anaheim green chiles plus 2 serranos with seeds.

8 Hatch (New Mexico green) chiles, seeded
5 tomatillos, husked and rinsed
4 plum tomatoes
1/2 onion, peeled
1/2 teaspoon sugar
1/4 teaspoon salt

Dry-roast the chiles, tomatillos, tomatoes, and onion in a hot skillet over medium heat for 10 to 15 minutes, doing it in batches if need be. Shake the pan occasionally to roast them all evenly and take care not to blacken. Roughly chop and transfer them to a blender, along with the sugar and salt, and purée until completely smooth.

Serving suggestions: This salsa goes well with vegetables and lighter-flavored foods, such as eggs, chicken, and seafood. It is especially good with posole.

Storage: Store in the refrigerator and use within 2 or 3 days.

Preparation time: About 25 minutes

Yield: About 3 cups

CHIMAYO RED CHILE SALSA

Chimayo is a small Hispanic community nestled in the Sangre de Cristo mountains north of Santa Fe. While its name is derived from a Tewa Indian word, tsimayo, *referring to the local stone, Chimayo was settled by the Spanish back in the seventeenth century and it retains a strong sense of its history and heritage. It is famous for its* Santuario, *or church, whose spring water and mud are said to have miraculous healing powers. It is also justly renowned for its ripened New Mexico chiles; the altitude, soil, and climate produce a wonderfully refined yet earthy variety that is prized for its premium quality and unique flavor. Much of the crop is dried and woven into* ristras, *long strings of ripened red chiles, which are hung up to dry against the brown adobe walls beneath the cloudless, azure fall sky. This provides one of the most vivid seasonal images of the Southwest. This is a robust, country-style salsa: its texture and intensity are part of its charm.*

8 ounces (about 25) dried Chimayo (New Mexico red) chiles, with seeds
4 cloves roasted garlic, peeled and finely minced
I teaspoon salt
I tablespoon dried oregano, toasted and ground

Toast the chiles, and rehydrate them in 2 quarts water (page 120). Drain the chiles, reserving 2 cups of the water. Place the chiles in a blender. If it is not bitter, add the reserved chile water. Otherwise add 2 cups of plain water. Add the garlic and salt to the blender and purée. Stir in the oregano, and warm it slightly, if desired.

Serving suggestions: Can be served warm with steak or grilled and roasted meats, grilled shrimp, and enchiladas; or at room temperature as a dip, with tortilla chips.

Storage: Keeps well in the refrigerator for weeks, and can also be frozen.

Preparation time: About 40 minutes

Yield: About 3 cups

CHILE CONFETTI

As its name suggests, this is a colorful salsa. If you want to raise the heat quotient a little, you can substitute a fresh (or pickled) Scotch bonnet or habanero chile for the serranos. Try to dice the ingredients as evenly and as finely as possible.

½ red bell pepper, seeded and minced
½ yellow bell pepper, seeded and minced
2 serrano chiles, seeded and minced
4 shallots, peeled and minced
¼ cup unseasoned rice vinegar
I teaspoon salt
2 tablespoons fresh lime juice
I teaspoon sugar
2 tablespoons virgin olive oil
I tablespoon chopped fresh chives
I tablespoon chopped fresh cilantro leaves

In a sieve, rinse the bell peppers and serranos under cold water until the water runs clear. (This process helps to keep the confetti clear.) Dry on paper towels, and transfer to a mixing bowl. Add the shallots, vinegar, salt, lime juice, and sugar, and thoroughly mix together. Whisk in the olive oil and garnish with the chives and cilantro.

Serving suggestions: The perfect accompaniment for fresh oysters on the half shell and other raw shellfish, or try it with fish tacos. Should be served chilled.

Storage: Best used the same day, but will hold for 1 day if necessary.

Variation: To make a salad dressing, whisk in about ½ cup additional virgin olive oil.

Preparation time: About 20 minutes

Yield: About 1½ cups

FIRE-ROASTED TOMATO CHIPOTLE SALSA

One of the essential features of Southwestern foods is a smoky, earthy aroma and flavor. This quality is undoubtedly linked to the age-old traditions of cooking over open fires and in hornos, *wood-burning brick or adobe ovens. Though our tools may be somewhat different, we can still practice these traditional methods today. Modern techniques of smoking foods and grilling over hard woods can yield the same satisfying, traditional flavors, and at the same time reconnect us with nature and a simpler time and lifestyle.*

16 ripe plum tomatoes (about 2 pounds)
¼ cup plus 1 tablespoon virgin olive oil
½ onion, peeled and chopped
4 cloves roasted garlic, peeled and finely minced
½ cup minced fresh cilantro leaves
4 chipotle chiles en adobo, chopped
¼ cup red wine vinegar
1 tablespoon salt
1 teaspoon sugar

Blacken half the tomatoes on a rack over a gas burner, over a grill, or with a hand-held butane torch (available from hardware stores). Heat a tablespoon of olive oil in a sauté pan over medium heat until lightly smoking, add the onion, and sauté until caramelized, about 10 minutes. Transfer the onion, blackened tomatoes, and garlic to a food processor or blender, and pulse until finely chopped but not puréed. Add the cilantro and chipotle chiles, and pulse again to mix.

Peel, seed, and chop the remaining pound of tomatoes, and fold in together with the vinegar, the remaining ¼ cup olive oil, salt, and sugar.

Serving suggestions: Serve at room temperature as an all-purpose salsa. It's proved so popular that we now sell it at the Coyote Cafe General Store.

Storage: It will hold well for up to 4 or 5 days in the refrigerator.

Variation: Substitute 2 pounds of tomatillos for the tomatoes. Husk and rinse the tomatillos, and roast them before using.

Preparation time: About 45 minutes

Yield: About 4 cups

WILD MUSHROOM AND SUN-DRIED TOMATO SALSA

Preserved foods are an important element in South-western cuisine. For thousands of years, Native Americans of the region have dried corn, squash, chiles, and meats for use during the winter, and their techniques were later adopted by the Spanish missionaries. Thus, contrary to popular belief, sun-dried tomatoes originated in the New World, and not in Italy!

Wild mushrooms abound in the Sangre de Cristo mountains above Santa Fe, especially after the spring and summer thunderstorms. They were gathered extensively by the Native Americans throughout the Southwest and used in a variety of dishes. The woodsiness of the wild mushrooms mixed with the intense tones of the sun-dried tomatoes gives this dish wonderful depth and density of flavors.

Note: The mushrooms can be grilled and the tomatoes rehydrated ahead of time. If you enjoy the grilled flavor, you can also grill the shallots. Use tomatoes that come in dried, packaged form rather than sun-dried tomatoes packed in oil. You can substitute 3 oven-roasted plum tomatoes for the sun-dried tomatoes.

⅓ **cup sun-dried tomatoes (about 1 ounce), not oil-packed**

8 **ounces fresh chanterelles, oyster mushrooms, or other wild mushrooms**

¼ **teaspoon salt**

4 **tablespoons virgin olive oil**

4 **shallots, peeled and minced**

2 **tablespoons balsamic vinegar**

¼ **teaspoon brown sugar**

1 **tablespoon minced fresh basil leaves**

Rehydrate the sun-dried tomatoes in warm water for about 30 minutes. Drain and chop them, and set them aside. Prepare the grill. Wash the mushrooms and drain them, shaking off as much water as you can. While they are still damp, sprinkle them with salt. Pour 2 tablespoons of the olive oil in a bowl, add the mushrooms, and toss well. Grill the mushrooms evenly until lightly browned but not too soft, brushing with the remaining 2 tablespoons olive oil. Chop the mushrooms into ⅜-inch dice and transfer to a mixing bowl. Combine with the sun-dried tomatoes, shallots, vinegar, and sugar. Add the basil immediately before serving.

Serving suggestions: Serve at room temperature with grilled fish such as tuna, halibut, and sea bass, with grilled poultry or steaks, or with pasta or on pizza. This salsa also makes an excellent relleno filling or, mixed with a little wild rice, a stuffing for quail.

Storage: This salsa keeps well for days in an airtight container in the refrigerator.

Variation: For a spicy version, add ½ teaspoon chile caribe and 1 teaspoon of chipotle chile purée (page 120), or substitute 4 tablespoons Chile Oil (page 40) for the olive oil.

Preparation time: About 45 minutes

Yield: About 2 cups

SALSA DE CALABAZA

Calabaza, *or squash, was one of the most important food crops in Native American agriculture, so important that it was once considered a sacred plant. All forms of calabaza are indigenous to the New World: in fact, archaeological evidence shows that squash was cultivated at least 7,500 years ago in Mexico. It is probable that it was the oldest cultivated staple of Mesoamerica, predating beans, chiles, and corn. Squash was grown by the Pueblo Indians of the Southwest at least 2,000 years ago, and probably well before that.*

This is a great example of a simple vegetable salsa that can also be used as a vegetable side dish. The secret to this recipe is to select young, tender, freshly harvested squash; do not use old, overly large squash, as they have too many seeds, and don't use baby squash, as they lack sufficient flavor.

½ **small red onion, peeled and cut into** ⅛-**inch dice**
1 **small zucchini, ends trimmed**
1 **small yellow summer squash, ends trimmed**
1 **small carrot, peeled**
2 **tomatillos, husked and rinsed**
1 **medium tomato**
3 **serrano chiles, seeded and minced**
2 **tablespoons minced fresh marjoram leaves**
¼ **cup extra-virgin olive oil**
1 **tablespoon unseasoned rice vinegar**
Sugar to taste
Salt to taste

Place the onion in a strainer, rinse with hot water, and drain. Cut the squashes, carrot, tomatillos, and tomato as neatly as possible into ⅛-inch dice. Place them in a mixing bowl along with the onion and all the remaining ingredients, and mix thoroughly. Let sit for at least 1 hour before serving to allow the flavors to combine. Strain off some of the excess juice immediately before serving.

Serving suggestions: Serve at room temperature as an accompaniment for sautéed or grilled fish and chicken; or cold, with tortilla chips.

Variation: Add 1 or 2 more serranos or 2 diced chipotle chiles *en adobo* for an extra-hot salsa.

Preparation time: About 30 minutes

Yield: About 2 cups

GAZPACHO SALSA

When I think of gazpacho, I recall the many versions I had on a horseback riding trip I made across southern Spain. In order not to subject the horses to the fierce heat of the midday sun, each day we'd stop at a small country inn along the way for two to three hours for lunch, shade, and a little siesta. At each of these posadas, *as they are called, we'd be served a cool vegetable gazpacho with crusty white bread for the first course; it was always light and refreshing, and stimulated the appetite. This salsa, with its fresh chopped garden vegetables, is a direct adaptation of those summertime soups. It is cooling and makes a great foil for spicy or rich food, especially on a hot summer day.*

2 **tomatillos, husked and rinsed**
1 **large ripe tomato**
½ **cucumber, peeled**
½ **large red bell pepper, seeded**
½ **large yellow bell pepper, seeded**
¼ **medium red onion, peeled**
1 **serrano chile with seeds, minced**
1 **clove garlic, peeled and finely minced (optional)**
2 **tablespoons minced fresh cilantro leaves, or basil, dill, or chives**
2 **tablespoons extra-virgin olive oil**
2 **tablespoons sherry vinegar, preferably Spanish**
¼ **teaspoon salt**

Cut the tomatillos, tomato, cucumber, bell pepper, and onion into ½-inch dice, as neatly as possible. Thoroughly combine them with all the other ingredients in a mixing bowl. Let sit at least 1 hour in the refrigerator before using to allow the flavors to combine. Strain off some of the excess juice immediately before serving.

Serving suggestions: Serve as a garnish for grilled fish, shrimp and lobster, cold soups, and fresh squash blossoms.

Storage: Best used the same day or the tomatoes and cucumbers become watery and soggy.

Preparation time: About 30 minutes

Yield: About 2 ¼ cups

HOTTER-THAN-HELL RED AND GREEN HABANERO SALSA

The small, lantern-shaped habanero is particularly deceptive in appearance: it looks like a miniature bell pepper, and you would expect it to be quite mild, but it packs a volcanic explosion of fiery heat. In fact, of all the known chiles in the world, the habanero is the hottest. It is native to the Caribbean basin, which includes the Yucatán region of Mexico; it ranges in color from green to yellow, orange, and red. Whatever its color, a little goes a long way! In addition to their intense heat, habanero chiles have a wonderful distinctive flavor with tropical fruit tones that perfectly complement foods containing fruit such as mangoes, papayas, and pineapple.

There are several condiment sauces on the market made with habanero chiles, and they too should be used sparingly. I use them all the time – a drop or two added to a sauce or soup perks up the other flavors and adds a lot of rhythm to a dish.

Note: Be sure to wear plastic gloves when handling the feisty little habaneros, and be careful not to touch your face – especially your eyes. If fresh habaneros are not available, use 2 dried habaneros, pulsed in a spice mill.

1 red habanero chile, seeded and cut into ⅛-inch dice
1 green habanero chile, seeded and cut into ⅛-inch dice
1 red bell pepper, seeded and cut into ⅛-inch dice
1 mango, peeled, pitted, and cut into ¼-inch dice
2 scallions, green and white parts, minced
2 tablespoons fresh lime juice
2 tablespoons Myers's dark Jamaican rum (optional)
1 teaspoon unseasoned rice vinegar
1 teaspoon peeled and minced fresh ginger
1 teaspoon salt
½ teaspoon sugar

Thoroughly combine all the ingredients in a mixing bowl. Let the salsa sit in the refrigerator for 30 minutes before serving to allow the flavors to combine.

Serving suggestions: Serve chilled or at room temperature with grilled fish or chicken. For real fire-breathers, this salsa can also be used to accompany pork served with the Mango Scotch Bonnet Caribbean Barbecue Glaze (page 86).

Storage: Best used the same day for optimum flavor.

Preparation time: About 20 minutes

Yield: About 1¾ cups

SONORA CACTUS SALSA

The Sonoran desert south of Tucson is one of the most beautiful places in the late spring when it comes to life after the long sleep of the winter months. Wildflowers magically appear and form a fuzzy, colorful blanket that contrasts dramatically with the austere landscape, and the nopales cactus takes on succulent new growth. The paddles of the nopales or prickly pear cactus traditionally were harvested by the Native Americans of that region and were an important food in their diet.

In Mexico, use of the nopales cactus goes back a long way, too. It is recorded that when the Spanish conquistadors first ate the cactus in Mexico, they fell ill. Don't worry – this is not a typical reaction! Most people wonder what cactus tastes like; its flavor is a cross between okra and green beans; when used raw, it has a firm, crunchy texture. But remember: cactus is very difficult to eat unless you first remove the spines!

Note: Both the cactus pad and the cactus syrup, which is derived from the *tuna*, or fruit of the cactus, are available at Latin markets, as is pomegranate juice. You can also substitute a mixture of unsweetened cherry and blackberry juice for the prickly pear syrup.

2 tomatillos
1 red bell pepper, halved and seeded
½ yellow bell pepper, seeded
1½ cups small nopales (about 2 pads, 6 inches long)
2 serrano chiles, seeded and finely minced
¼ cup prickly pear syrup or pomegranate juice
1½ tablespoons juice from canned chipotle chiles en adobo
2 tablespoons minced fresh cilantro leaves
2 tablespoons roasted corn kernels (page 120)
1 tablespoon minced fresh spearmint leaves, or peppermint
¼ teaspoon salt

Remove the husks from the tomatillos, and save them. Rinse the tomatillos and cut them and the red and yellow bell peppers into ¼-inch dice. If the needles have not been removed from the cactus pads, put on a pair of thick gloves and remove them with a long knife. Cut around the edges to remove the fine quills there. Bring a small panful of water to a boil, add the tomatillo husks, and blanch the cactus for 1 minute (the husks prevent the cactus from getting slimy and from losing color). Drain the cactus and plunge it into ice water. When cool, cut into 1-inch by ¼-inch strips. Combine all the ingredients in a mixing bowl and let sit for 1 hour before using to allow the flavors to combine.

Serving suggestions: This salsa can be served cold as a side salad with chilled roasted meats or poached shrimp, or as a garnish for barbecued meats. It's also good hot, with tortillas, or to accompany grilled meats (especially lamb) or scrambled eggs.

Storage: Best served the same day as the color will fade and the cactus can become stringy.

Variation: The cactus can be grilled, in which case, blanching is unnecessary. For a simpler salsa, combine the nopales with orange segments and diced red onion.

Preparation time: About 30 minutes

Yield: About 2 cups

TROPICAL FRUIT SALSA

Fruits, with their natural sweetness, are a perfect foil for and complement to foods with very intense tastes. At the same time, they have a refreshing and somewhat acidic quality that cuts through fried foods and foods with rich textures. A good fruit salsa will contain a myriad of colors, flavors, and textures. In this recipe, we use pineapple for its acidity, the deep orange mango for its sweet lushness, the papaya for its golden richness, the red bell pepper for its color and crunch, and mint for its refreshing flavor and contrasting green color. Tropical fruits are sweeter and more richly flavored and satisfyingly complex, compared to other fruits. I'm sure it must have been a sensual ripe tropical mango that tempted Eve, rather than a boring old apple!

Note: The success of this recipe depends on using ripe, sweet fruit. Mangoes and papayas are usually harvested green: they should be ripened in a paper bag at room temperature until they become orange-yellow or rose in color and exude an exotic, tropical perfume.

½ pineapple, peeled and cored
1 small mango, peeled and pitted
1 small papaya, peeled and seeded
½ red bell pepper, seeded
1 tablespoon chopped fresh mint leaves
1 scallion, green and white parts, sliced
½ tablespoon red wine vinegar
2 tablespoons fresh orange juice
1 tablespoon fresh lime juice
½ tablespoon peeled and finely grated fresh ginger
½ teaspoon salt
½ teaspoon light brown sugar

Cut the pineapple, mango, papaya, and bell pepper into ¼-inch dice. Mix all the ingredients together in a mixing bowl. Let stand in the refrigerator for 30 minutes before serving to allow the flavors to combine.

Serving suggestions: Serve chilled with crunchy empanadas or savory cinnamon tamales, or with the simple flavors of plainly grilled chicken, mahi-mahi, shrimp, or lobster. Also good with ribs, and with grilled or jerked pork.

Storage: Best served the same day; this salsa does not keep well.

Variations: Add 2 tablespoons grated coconut and/or ¼ cup fresh coconut milk. For a spicy salsa, add 1 teaspoon seeded and minced fresh habanero chile.

Preparation time: About 30 minutes

Yield: About 2 cups

TANGY CITRUS SALSA

I'm a great believer in using more fruits as a flavoring ingredient; they can reduce the need for salt in foods because of their high natural acidity and flavor. In this salsa, the citrus fruits and the pineapple have vibrant, assertive flavors that successfully complement many foods. When making fruit salsas, take the play of color into consideration: for example, a mixture of pink and white grapefruit with a little persimmon makes for a striking presentation.

Note: Ripe pineapples have a strong aroma and feel slightly soft; the leaves should come away from the crown when pulled. Use an aged (*añejo*) 100 percent agave tequila, such as El Tesoro, for premium quality.

1 ripe pineapple, peeled and cored
1 grapefruit, peeled and sectioned
2 oranges, peeled and sectioned
2 limes, peeled
1 lemon, peeled
2 tablespoons chopped fresh cilantro leaves
2 tablespoons sugar
½ teaspoon salt
1 teaspoon cayenne chile powder
1 jigger (3 tablespoons) tequila

Cut the pineapple, grapefruit, oranges, limes, and lemon into ¼-inch dice. Combine them with the remaining ingredients in a mixing bowl and refrigerate.

Serving suggestions: Serve chilled with pork or highly flavored fish such as mackerel.

Storage: Best used the same day, for peak freshness.

Variation: Substitute tangerines for the oranges when in season.

Preparation time: About 20 minutes

Yield: About 3 cups

MANGO JÍCAMA SALSA

Jícama is an edible tuber that is also known as the Mexican potato. Like the potato, it has a brown skin and white flesh. It is sweet and crispy, rather like water chestnuts, and it has a cooling and refreshing quality, like a sweet radish or the Japanese daikon. Use young jícama which has a smooth surface, measures 4 to 6 inches across, and feels heavy for its size; avoid older jícama, which is starchy and dry. In this recipe, the crunch of the jícama offsets the sweet lushness of the mango, while the cilantro and lime juice add zesty tones.

8 ounces fresh jícama, peeled and cut into ¼-inch dice
½ ripe mango, peeled, pitted, and cut into ¼-inch dice
½ red bell pepper, seeded and cut into ⅛-inch dice
½ yellow bell pepper, seeded and cut into ⅛-inch dice
1 scallion, green part only, finely chopped
1 serrano chile, seeded and minced
2 tablespoons fresh lime juice
1 tablespoon finely chopped fresh cilantro leaves
1 tablespoon finely chopped fresh mint leaves
½ tablespoon peeled and finely minced fresh ginger
½ tablespoon unseasoned rice vinegar
½ tablespoon virgin olive oil
½ teaspoon sugar
Salt to taste
Freshly ground black pepper to taste

Combine all the ingredients in a mixing bowl and toss together. This relish should be a little sweet and a little sour; add more vinegar, lime juice, or sugar as necessary.

Serving suggestions: Serve at room temperature with grilled chicken, tuna, or mahimahi.

Storage: Best used the same day or the fruit becomes mushy and the jícama soft.

Preparation time: About 30 minutes

Yield: About 2½ cups

RIO GRANDE MELON SALSA

A hidden secret of the Southwest is that the sweetest melons in the country are grown right here in New Mexico and Texas. Our melons are justifiably considered to be even better than those grown in California or in the south of France. At Coyote Cafe, we use a variety of melons, including white Ogens, orange cantaloupes, and pale green honeydews and Crenshaws, all supplied to us by the Estancia Dos Rocas farm in the Rio Grande Valley near El Paso. During the summer, we get deliveries to the back door of the restaurant twice a week, right off a flatbed truck laden with hundreds of vine-ripened melons. In this salsa, the ripe, sweet fruit and the chiles make a terrific combination.

Notes: If the melons are very, very sweet, you can add some pineapple for a little acidity and a crunchy texture. I think that once a melon is refrigerated, its flavor diminishes.

2 pounds assorted ripe melons, such as cantaloupe, honeydew, and Persian
½ red bell pepper, seeded, and cut into ¼-inch dice
2 serrano chiles with seeds, finely minced
2 tablespoons finely chopped fresh mint leaves
1 tablespoon unseasoned rice vinegar
2 tablespoons fresh lime juice
2 teaspoons sugar, or to taste, depending on the sweetness of the melons

Peel, seed, and cut the melons into ¼-inch dice (you should have about 4 cups diced melon in all). In a large mixing bowl, combine the melon and bell pepper with the serranos, mint, vinegar, and lime juice. Add the sugar. Let sit for 30 minutes in the refrigerator before serving to allow the flavors to combine.

Serving suggestions: Serve chilled with grilled fish, seafood cocktails, grilled shrimp salad, chicken fajitas, or pork. If you omit the serranos, the salsa can be served with sorbets.

Storage: Use the same day for peak freshness.

Preparation time: About 20 minutes

Yield: About 3 cups

EL PASTOR PINEAPPLE SALSA

Searing or grilling ripe fruits or vegetables makes them sweeter as the heat caramelizes the natural sugars and intensifies their flavor. Because it has a high sugar content, pineapple should be browned very slowly in a pan or on the grill, or it will caramelize too quickly and create a burned, acrid flavor. Only use fresh, ripe pineapple for this recipe; canned pineapple will not suffice.

This salsa is named after the Mexican dish called tacos al pastor, *which are made with pork that has been marinated in fresh pineapple juice and cooked on huge, vertical rotating spits, rather like the Greek lamb gyros. The slight smokiness and the dense tropical tones in this salsa make a great combination.*

1 very ripe pineapple, peeled and cut into ¼-inch thick slices
½ red bell pepper, seeded and cut into ¼-inch dice
2 teaspoons chipotle chile purée (page 120)
2 tablespoons fresh orange juice
1 tablespoon fresh lime juice
1 tablespoon finely minced fresh cilantro leaves
2 teaspoons light brown or natural cane sugar

Cut the pineapple slices in half and dry-sauté in a nonstick sauté pan over medium heat for 8 minutes per side, until caramelized and golden brown. Core the pineapple slices, cut into ¼-inch dice, and transfer to a mixing bowl. Add the bell pepper, chipotle purée, orange juice, lime juice, cilantro, and sugar, and combine thoroughly. Taste, and add more lime juice and chiles if desired.

Serving suggestions: Serve at room temperature with pork, grilled chicken, or grilled fish.

Storage: Best used the same day.

Variation: Mangoes or peaches can be substituted for the pineapple.

Preparation time: About 30 minutes

Yield: About 3 cups

CHILE de ÁRBOL-GRAPEFRUIT SALSA

Citrus fruit was brought to the New World by Europeans, but grapefruit is a relatively modern species that originated within the last 200 years. Grapefruit probably first grew in Jamaica either as a natural hybrid, or as a mutation. Texas is famous for its Ruby Red grapefruit, which is probably the best eating grapefruit available in the United States, especially during the winter months. Their beautiful deep carmine color is particularly striking. The chile de árbol (see page 25) is hot and flavorful; its hints of smokiness and grassiness complement the tartness of the grapefruit well.

2 grapefruits, preferably Ruby Red, peeled and sectioned
½ tablespoon finely ground dried chile de árbol
2 tablespoons unseasoned rice vinegar
1 tablespoon virgin olive oil
4 teaspoons sugar
¼ teaspoon salt
1 tablespoon minced fresh chives

Chop each grapefruit section into 2 to 3 pieces and lightly squeeze to extract about ¼ cup juice. Place sections and juice in a mixing bowl, and combine with the chile de árbol, vinegar, olive oil, sugar, and salt. Be careful not to overmix the salsa, or the grapefruit might break up. Add the chives last. If the mixture is too tart, add a little more sugar.

Serving suggestions: Serve at room temperature with grilled fish, lobster, or pork.

Storage: Best served the same day, as it does not keep well.

Preparation time: About 20 minutes

Yield: About 1 cup

CHIPS

Chips are a wonderful extracurricular, out-of-hours, anytime party food, whether they're served in a simple basket or bowl to accompany a cold beer or margarita in the humblest bar or cantina, or elegantly presented on fine china with perfect martinis and caviar. No matter how or where, chips, like the salsas they are so often served with, mean fun.

While many countries use a form of salsa as a condiment or flavoring element with their foods, chips are even more of an international favorite, and take a variety of forms all across the globe. Welcome to the World Pavilion of Chips where you can select anything from American potato chips and Southwestern-style barbecue or jalapeño corn tortilla chips and black bean chips, to Hawaiian taro chips, British chips seasoned with salt and vinegar, or Australian cheese and onion "crisps," South American plantain chips, to Japanese wasabi rice chips and Indonesian shrimp chips. The choice often seems endless, as you know if you've ever strolled through the snack section in your local supermarket.

Potato chips originated in the United States in the mid-1800s. Culinary legend has it that a fussy patron at Moon's Lake House in Saratoga Springs, a fashionable spa town in upstate New York, complained that the fried potatoes were sliced too thick. The chef, George Crum, responded by slicing the potatoes paper-thin, and these Saratoga potato chips soon became the rage all across the country (French fries became popular only at the end of the century).

Chips and salsas are an unbeatable combination, but for the ultimate snack, you should make your own salsas *and* your own chips. Chips are surprisingly easy to make at home, and, because you can use premium, fresh ingredients when you make your own, and eliminate additives such as MSG and preservatives, your homemade chips will be infinitely better than any you can buy. In addition, they will be much less expensive.

TIPS FOR MAKING GREAT CHIPS

- Authentic Mexican tortilla chips are fried in lard, which gives them their rich taste, but in today's nutrition-conscious environment it makes sense to use healthier, unsaturated oils as the cooking medium. Try a vegetable oil with a neutral flavor, such as canola, corn, peanut, or grapeseed oil. Olive oil and nut oils, with the exception of peanut oil, are unsuitable as they will impart too strong a flavor.

- Be sure to store your oils properly, and never use one that is even slightly rancid. While refined oils do not need to be refrigerated, they should be stored in a dark, cool place; most will keep for at least 6 months.

- Different oils have different smoking and combustion points, so adjust cooking temperatures accordingly. If the cooking temperature is too low, more oil will be absorbed, resulting in heavier, oilier chips. Grapeseed and peanut oils have very high smoking points and using either one of them will result in lighter, less oily chips.

- Use enough oil to maintain a high cooking temperature, thus ensuring that the oil is not absorbed by the chips.

- Season the chips while they are still warm.

- Liquid seasonings (lime juice, for instance) are best sprayed on with an atomizer. Get a 1-cup or smaller sprayer (available from nurseries or plant sections of hardware stores) and strain the juice first.

- Eat up homemade chips quickly – what the heck, someone has to do it – as they will become stale faster than commercial chips which are vacuum packed and usually contain preservatives.

PUEBLO BLUE CORN CHIPS

Blue corn has come into vogue lately, mostly as a curiosity item. Few people realize, though, that blue corn has been cultivated for thousands of years by Native Americans in the Southwest. While it was grown for food, it also held religious significance, and was used in ceremonial dances to honor the regeneration of Mother Earth. Blue corn is still grown by the Pueblo Indians of the region, and it remains an important part of the native New Mexican cuisine.

24 6-inch fresh blue corn tortillas
1 to 2 quarts peanut or vegetable oil, for frying
3 tablespoons fresh lime juice
1 teaspoon salt

Cut each tortilla into 8 triangles. Heat the oil in a deep fryer or large pot to 350 degrees. Fry the tortillas in batches for about 30 seconds, until crisp but not overcooked. Remove with a slotted spoon or use a spoon and strainer, and drain on paper towels. Transfer to a large bowl and while the chips are still warm, spray with the lime juice and sprinkle with salt.

Serving suggestions: For best results, serve immediately with a salsa, a black bean dip, or guacamole. The chips can also be served as nachos: top with melted cheese and garnish with chives.

Storage: Can be stored in a cool, dry place for 2 to 3 days, or up to 1 week in dry climates.

Preparation time: About 20 minutes

Yield: About 16 cups

ROUNDUP BARBECUE CHIPS

When you think of barbecue, you think of smoke, fire, and spice. Most barbecue chips disappoint on all three counts, but not these. Use the best quality chile powder you can find – it'll make all the difference.

24 6-inch fresh corn tortillas
1 to 2 quarts canola or vegetable oil, for frying
Chip Seasoning:
1½ tablespoons pure red chile powder
2 teaspoons ground dried chipotle chile
½ tablespoon finely ground dried oregano
¾ teaspoon finely ground cumin
½ tablespoon salt
¼ teaspoon cayenne chile powder

Cut each tortilla into 8 triangles. Heat the oil in a deep fryer or large pot to 350 degrees. Meanwhile, thoroughly combine all the chip seasoning ingredients in a mixing bowl. Fry the tortillas in batches for about 30 seconds, until crisp but not overcooked. Remove with a slotted spoon or use a spoon and strainer, and drain on paper towels. Transfer to a large bowl and toss chips with the chip seasoning while still warm.

Serving suggestions: For best results, serve immediately with a cooling accompaniment such as a salsa or a black bean dip. Also good as a side dish with lunch salads, soups, burgers, or grilled sausages. Makes great nachos, topped with melted cheese.

Storage: Can be stored in a cool, dry place for 2 to 3 days, or up to 1 week in dry climates.

Preparation time: About 20 minutes

Yield: About 16 cups

CAMPESINO TORTILLA CHIPS

*While the previous recipes use ready-made corn tor-
tillas for the chips, this recipe calls for homemade tortillas made from a flavored masa dough. Masa dough
is a Southwestern and Mexican staple that is used to
make corn tortillas and tamales. If you live in a city
that has a tortilla factory, you could buy prepared
masa dough there and flavor it yourself with chipotle
chile purée and cumin. Otherwise, follow the instruc-
tions below to make your own dough. To make the
tortillas, you will need a tortilla press, available from
Latin markets, specialty stores, or the Coyote Cafe
General Store (see page 123).*

1 cup masa harina
1 cup cornmeal
3 tablespoons unsalted butter, at room temperature
1¼ cups water
1 tablespoon fresh lime juice
½ teaspoon salt
¼ cup chipotle chile purée (page 120)
1 teaspoon finely ground cumin
1 to 2 quarts vegetable oil, for frying

Preheat the oven to 350 degrees. Place the masa
harina, cornmeal, butter, water, lime juice, salt,
chipotle purée, and cumin in the bowl of an electric
mixer and mix until smooth, scraping down the
sides of the bowl if necessary. Pinch off about 1½
tablespoons of the dough and roll it into a ball.
Open the tortilla press and place a sheet of plastic
wrap over the bottom half. Put the ball of dough in
the middle of the plastic wrap, flatten slightly with
your palm, and cover with another sheet of plastic
wrap. Close the tortilla press and flatten the dough
into a thin circle, about 4 to 5 inches across. Open
the press and gently remove the top layer of plastic
wrap. Invert the dough onto a clean surface and
gently peel back the remaining layer of plastic wrap.
Transfer the dough circle to a baking sheet lined
with parchment paper. Repeat for remaining dough
and place as many circles on the baking sheet as will
fit in a single layer. Bake in the preheated oven for 5
to 7 minutes, until crispy (do this in batches if necessary). Remove the baking sheet from the oven and
let the tortillas rest for 5 to 7 minutes.

Meanwhile, heat the oil in a deep fryer or large
pot to 350 degrees. Cut each cooled tortilla into 6
triangles, fry in batches for about 1 minute, until
crisp but not overcooked. Remove with a slotted
spoon or use a spoon and strainer, and drain on paper towels. Spray with a little extra lime juice and
sprinkle with salt, if desired.

Serving suggestions: For bests results, serve immediately with a salsa, or as a side dish with salads,
soups, or burgers.

Storage: Can be stored in a cool, dry place for 2 to
3 days, or up to 1 week in dry climates.

Preparation time: About 1 hour

Yield: About 20 cups

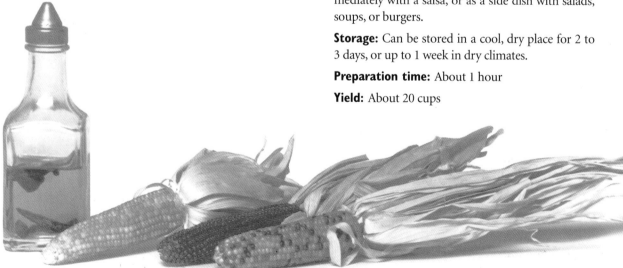

HOMEMADE RED CHILE POTATO CHIPS

When I was a child, I used to think that potato chips were one of the marvels of modern manufacturing and that they were created in a factory. We never made them at home, and none of the restaurants we visited ever served homemade potato chips. I had no idea they were related to the "real" potatoes – baked, boiled, or mashed – that we ate at home for dinner.

Of course I've since learned how easy they are to make. These particular chips are much better than store-bought spiced chips which usually contain MSG and other additives and preservatives. In addition, the chile powder you use will be fresher and of a higher quality, and you can adjust the spiciness to suit your own palate.

Note: Idaho russet baking potatoes make the best chips as they are high in moisture content and low in sugar.

**2 to 3 (about 1 pound) Idaho baking potatoes
1 to 2 quarts peanut or canola oil, for frying**

Chip Seasoning:

**¹⁄₂ teaspoon pure red chile powder
¹⁄₂ teaspoon cayenne chile powder
¹⁄₄ teaspoon salt**

Peel and slice the potatoes paper-thin with a mandolin or in a food processor. Soak the sliced potatoes in ice-cold water for 5 minutes. (You can slice the potatoes ahead of time and hold them in water for as long as 4 or 5 hours.) Drain in a salad spinner or lay flat on kitchen towels and pat dry.

Heat the oil in a deep fryer or large pot to 350 degrees. Meanwhile, thoroughly combine all the chip seasoning ingredients in a bowl. Fry the potatoes in batches until crisp and brown. Remove with a slotted spoon or use a spoon and strainer, and drain on paper towels. Transfer to a large bowl and toss chips with the chip seasoning while still warm.

Serving suggestions: For best results, serve immediately. Good with burgers, sandwiches, or with eggs and chorizo for breakfast or brunch.

Storage: Can be stored in a cool, dry place for 2 to 3 days, or up to 1 week in dry climates.

Preparation time: About 25 minutes

Yield: About 8 cups

YUCATÁN PLANTAIN CHIPS

Plantains are members of the banana family: they are starchier and less sweet than regular bananas, and are never eaten raw. They are a common ingredient in Caribbean cuisines, where they are often served as a starch, much as rice or potatoes would be served in other cuisines. Plantains are cooked at all stages of ripeness, but for this recipe, they should be bought green and allowed to ripen until the skins begin to turn black.

These chips take on a distinctive orange color when they are fried, and are very decorative as they curl up on themselves if they have been sliced thinly enough.

**2 pounds ripe plantains
¹⁄₂ dried habanero chile, ground (about ¹⁄₄ teaspoon), or ¹⁄₂ teaspoon cayenne chile powder or ground dried chile de árbol
¹⁄₂ teaspoon salt
1 teaspoon sugar
2 quarts vegetable oil, for frying**

Using a mandolin, electric slicer, or hand-held vegetable slicer, cut the plantains very thinly lengthwise. Combine the ground habanero, salt, and sugar in a small bowl and set aside. Heat the oil in a deep-fryer or large pot to 350 degrees. Fry the plantains in batches until crisp and light brown, about 30 seconds. Remove with a slotted spoon or use a spoon and strainer, and drain on paper towels. Transfer to a large bowl and toss with the seasoning mix while still warm.

Serving suggestions: Plantain chips are ideal for buffets. They go very well with tropical fruit salsas and black beans, and can also be used as a starch for a main course.

Storage: Store in a cool, dry place for 3 to 4 days.

Preparation time: About 10 minutes

Yield: About 4 to 6 servings

CHUTNEYS, RELISHES, AND PICKLES

Like their cousins the salsas, chutneys, relishes, and pickles can provide wonderful taste accents or "counterpoints" for any meal. These flavorful accompaniments are also multipurpose, and in addition to filling their primary role as condiments, they can be used as sides, spreads, sauces, or even pizza toppings. In general, chutneys, relishes, and pickles hold much longer than salsas, so you can keep an assortment on reserve in the refrigerator or the pantry, and pull them out for unexpected company or pack them as a last-minute addition for picnics or cook-outs.

Chutneys originated in India (the word comes from the Hindi *chatni*). Traditionally, they are made from fresh or dried fruit, nuts, vinegar, sugar, and spices. Chutneys have a thick texture that can be either chunky or smooth, and they range in heat from mild to hot. Their sweetness enlivens and provides a contrast to other foods.

Relishes are similar to chutneys except that they are usually made with diced fresh fruits or vegetables. A really zesty relish can be used to add zip to bland foods, while the milder ones combine particularly well with spicy foods. Relishes were first produced commercially in the United States by Henry Heinz in the late 1800s.

Pickling entails preserving foods, from meat and fish to vegetables and fruit, in a salt water or vinegar brine. Pickled foods have been around for centuries, and can be found in some form in every corner of the world. China has its pickled eggs and ginger, Korea its kim chee, Mexico its jalapeños *en escabeche*, Germany its dills. History records that Cleopatra valued pickles as a beauty aid, and that Thomas Jefferson regarded them as a favorite comfort food. Nowadays you can find pickled eggs, herring, and pigs' feet, as well as cucumbers (the most common pickled item), onions, chiles, baby corn, beans, beets, okra, and cauliflower, to name but a few of the ingredients that lend themselves to the pickling process. Pickles are wonderfully adaptable—they can be made sweet, sour, tangy, or hot.

Preparing chutneys, relishes, and pickles at home is easy to do, and you will find that the ones you make yourself are far superior even to the gourmet store-bought versions. You can make them with less salt and sugar, fewer preservatives, and higher-quality ingredients. These condiments are best put up during the summer and early fall when fruits and vegetables are running riot in the garden and when they are inexpensive at the markets and roadside stands. Use the freshest ingredients you can, and never use bruised or blemished produce. When pickling, use soft or distilled water, as hard water can result in cloudy liquid.

In preparing chutneys, relishes, and pickles, you should use nonreactive equipment (stainless steel, glass, enamel, etc.). All these recipes should be stored in the refrigerator. Use airtight containers: for a colorful and practical presentation, try glass apothecary jars with cork or glass stoppers.

CHILE DE ÁRBOL-APRICOT CHUTNEY

Chile de árbol *literally means "treelike chile," and this chile is so named because it grows on lush plants with thick, woody stems. It is bright brick red, about 2 to 3 inches long, and is usually sold in dried form. Like the cayenne chile, to which it is related, the árbol has a very fiery heat. It is notable for a deep fruitiness and smoky tones, which makes it a good match for fruit such as apricots. Orchards of soft fruit, notably apricots, peaches, cherries, and plums, were planted by Hispanic settlers in the upper Rio Grande Valley of northern New Mexico where Pueblo Indians had farmed for centuries. Canned, bottled, and preserved fruit provided welcome relief to the winter diet of dried and stored staples such as corn, potatoes, and grains.*

I teaspoon virgin olive oil

¼ white onion, peeled and minced

I tablespoon peeled and grated fresh ginger

1½ teaspoons roughly ground chile de árbol

¼ teaspoon ground allspice

½ cup sugar

½ teaspoon salt

I cup unseasoned rice vinegar

1½ pounds fresh apricots, pitted, and cut into ⅛-inch dice (about 3 cups)

I cup water

I tablespoon chopped fresh mint leaves

In a stainless steel or other nonreactive saucepan, heat the olive oil and sauté the onion over medium heat until soft, about 5 minutes. Stir in the ginger, chile de árbol, and allspice, making sure there are no lumps. Add the sugar and salt, and deglaze the pan with the vinegar. Bring to a boil, and then reduce heat to a simmer. Add the apricots and cook until the mixture thickens, about 10 minutes. Remove the pan from heat, add the water, let cool, and then stir in the mint.

Serving suggestions: Serve cold or at room temperature with grilled fish and shellfish, or pork ribs.

Storage: Stores well in the refrigerator for up to 2 weeks in airtight jars.

Variation: This recipe can be made with dry, preferably unsulphured, apricots (soak 1 pound dried apricots in warm water for about 20 minutes and proceed with the recipe). You can also substitute fresh nectarines or peaches. If chiles de árbol are unavailable, substitute with dried cayenne chiles.

Preparation time: About 40 minutes

Yield: About 4 cups

NEW MEXICO GREEN CHILE CHUTNEY

The idea of making chutney with green chiles is natural, given their abundance in the fall, and the fact that they marry well with so many other flavors. The heat of the chiles provides balance as well as depth to counter the sweetness of the sugar. The spiciness of this chutney will depend on how hot the chiles are, so adjust according to taste. Like many other chutneys and relishes, this recipe makes a wonderful sandwich spread if reduced a little to thicken it up.

2 tablespoons virgin olive oil
1 tablespoon peeled and minced white onion
2 cloves garlic, peeled and finely minced
1/2 tablespoon peeled and grated fresh ginger
6 New Mexico or Anaheim green chiles, roasted, peeled, seeded, and cut into 1/8-inch dice
6 jalapeño chiles, roasted, peeled, seeded, and cut into 1/8-inch dice
1/2 cup sugar
3/4 teaspoon finely ground dried oregano
1/2 teaspoon ground cinnamon
1/2 teaspoon salt
1 cup cider vinegar

In a stainless steel or other nonreactive saucepan, heat the oil and sauté the onion, garlic, and ginger for 5 minutes. Add the chiles, sugar, oregano, cinnamon, and salt, and cook for 10 minutes longer, stirring to make sure the sugar is dissolved. Deglaze the pan with the vinegar and cook until thickened, about 10 minutes. Let cool.

Serving suggestions: Serve at room temperature with lamb chops or crab cakes. Use as a spread in chicken, turkey, lamb, pork, or goat cheese sandwiches, or as a substitute for plain pickle relish.

Storage: Holds well in the refrigerator for weeks.

Variation: This recipe can be made just as well with fresh, ripe, red chiles, which will result in a sweeter chutney.

Preparation time: About 1 hour

Yield: About 3 cups

CHILE PASADO APPLE CHUTNEY

This recipe uses both roasted fresh green chiles and chile pasado, the New Mexico red or Anaheim red chile that has been roasted, peeled, and dried. This is a traditional method of preserving chiles that has been used for centuries by the Native Americans of the Southwest. Dried chiles were an important source of vitamins for these peoples, especially vitamin C.
The flavor of green chiles matches apples well: both are grown in the upper Rio Grande Valley of northern New Mexico around Velarde and Dixon. The chile pasado is best ground in a spice mill or coffee grinder.

1 tablespoon peanut oil
1/4 medium onion, peeled and minced
2 teaspoons dried oregano
2 New Mexico or Anaheim green chiles, roasted, peeled, seeded, and cut into 1/8-inch dice
2 tablespoons roughly ground chile pasado, or 1 large poblano chile, roasted, peeled, seeded, and cut into 1/8-inch dice
2 red Fresno chiles, or 2 red jalapeños, seeded and minced
2 tablespoons sugar
1/4 cup cider vinegar
1 1/2 cups fresh apple cider, preferably unfiltered
3 Granny Smith apples, peeled, cored, and cut into 1/4-inch dice

In a medium stainless steel or other nonreactive saucepan, heat the peanut oil and sauté the onion over medium heat until translucent, about 5 minutes. Add the oregano and stir to toast slightly. Stir in the green chiles, chile pasado, Fresnos or jalapeños, and sugar. Deglaze the pan with the vinegar and apple cider, and reduce the liquid by half. Add the apples and simmer 5 minutes longer. The mixture should be fairly thick but the apples should not be too soft. Let cool.

Serving suggestions: Serve at room temperature with roasted poultry, or game.

Storage: Keeps in the refrigerator for up to 1 week.

Variation: If fresh green chiles are unavailable, use frozen (see Source List, page 123) but do not roast them.

Preparation time: About 45 minutes

Yield: About 4 cups

TOMMY'S SUNBURST GINGER CHUTNEY

Ginger is a pungent, aromatic rhizome; it is indigenous to Southeast Asia, but has a long history of use worldwide. It was popular in ancient Rome as well as in medieval Europe, and was brought to North America by the British in colonial days. It is used in tandem with chiles in a number of cuisines, including the Indian, Szechuan, Hunan, Thai, and Caribbean styles of cooking. In this recipe, the ginger provides a clear and strong flavor that is complemented perfectly by the bell peppers, which are the mildest form of chiles. Tommy Birdwell, a line chef at Coyote Cafe, helped develop this recipe.

1 teaspoon virgin olive oil
2 red bell peppers, seeded and cut into ¼-inch dice
2 yellow bell peppers, seeded and cut into ¼-inch dice
½ tablespoon peeled and grated fresh ginger
½ cup sugar
¼ teaspoon salt
1 cup cider vinegar

Heat the olive oil in a pan and sauté the bell peppers and ginger over medium heat for 5 minutes. Add the sugar and salt, stir in the vinegar, and cook for 10 to 15 minutes longer, until the mixture thickens.

Serving suggestions: Serve warm over lamb or pork, with smoked salmon, or stir into rice for an interesting twist.

Storage: Holds well in the refrigerator for weeks.

Preparation time: About 45 minutes

Yield: About 2 cups

MINTY MANGO CHUTNEY

This is a refreshing variation on the classic mango chutney that is a standby of Indian cuisine. Store-bought mango chutneys tend to be too heavily spiced, which is a shame, as the natural flavor of the mango is overpowered. In this recipe, the rich, fruity lushness of the mango is preserved by keeping cooking time to a minimum and by using seasonings sparingly. The mango is perfectly complemented by the tang of ginger and the refreshing taste of mint. The best time to make this is in the late spring and summer, which is the peak of the mango season in the United States.

1 tablespoon peanut oil
2 medium shallots, peeled and minced
1 tablespoon peeled and grated fresh ginger
2 mangoes, peeled, pitted, and cut into ¼-inch dice
½ cup sugar
1 tablespoon chile caribe
½ cup champagne vinegar
½ cup julienned fresh mint leaves
1 teaspoon salt

In a stainless steel or other nonreactive pan, heat the peanut oil and sauté the shallot and ginger over medium heat until translucent, about 5 minutes. Add the mangoes, sugar, and chile caribe, and sauté until tender but not mushy, about 5 minutes longer. Deglaze the pan with the vinegar and reduce the liquid until the ingredients have thickened, about 3 to 5 minutes. Fold in the mint and salt. Let cool.

Serving suggestions: Serve cold or at room temperature with fish and poultry. This chutney can also be warmed in the microwave, but keep the heat low so that the sugars do not caramelize.

Storage: Keeps for weeks refrigerated in airtight jars.

Preparation time: About 45 minutes

Yield: About 2 cups

RIPE PEACH CONSERVE

Most people find it hard to believe that orchard fruit grows in the Southwest, but many of the river valleys here are protected from the wind and frosts, giving them a long growing season and a climate that is favorable for growing fruit. Only use ripe peaches for this recipe: they should be intensely fragrant and slightly soft to the touch. Avoid buying peaches with soft or brown spots, or any green markings. Peaches are in peak supply in early summer.

4 ripe peaches
I tablespoon unsalted butter
I onion, peeled and sliced
$\frac{1}{2}$ cup good-quality bourbon
$\frac{1}{2}$ cup water
$\frac{1}{2}$ cup light brown sugar
Juice of 2 oranges
Juice of 2 large lemons
I tablespoon molasses
I stick cinnamon
$\frac{1}{4}$ teaspoon salt

To peel the peaches, blanch them in boiling water for about 30 seconds and plunge them into ice water; the skins should slip off easily. Pit and slice the peaches. In a saucepan, heat the butter and sauté the onion over medium-high heat until caramelized, about 7 to 10 minutes. Add the peaches along with the remaining ingredients, lower the heat, and simmer until the mixture thickens.

Serving suggestions: Serve warm with grilled pork or chicken. Can also be puréed when cool and used as a glaze for meats.

Storage: Keeps well in the refrigerator for several weeks. Store in sealed jars.

Preparation time: About 45 minutes

Yield: About 2½ cups

TOMATILLO CHUTNEY

Tomatillos make an interesting base for a chutney. They have a fruity flavor that is like a combination of rhubarb, apple, plum, and lemon; they also have a sweet tartness as well as natural acidity and a high pectin content. Pectin is a natural thickening agent that is commonly used in commercial jams and preserves. This recipe is a variation of the more common tomato chutney, with the tomatillos providing a more vibrant color and tantalizing flavor.

I pound tomatillos, husked, rinsed, and cut into $\frac{1}{4}$-inch dice
I red bell pepper, seeded and cut into $\frac{1}{8}$-inch dice
I jalapeño chile, seeded and cut into $\frac{1}{8}$-inch dice
$\frac{1}{4}$ cup sugar
$\frac{1}{4}$ teaspoon salt
$\frac{1}{2}$ cup unseasoned rice vinegar
Zest of I lemon

Place the tomatillos, bell pepper, jalapeño, sugar, and salt in a saucepan and cook over medium heat for 3 minutes. Deglaze the pan with the vinegar and simmer for 10 minutes. Remove pan from heat, stir in the lemon zest, and let cool.

Serving suggestions: An excellent accompaniment for hot and spicy food, as well as chicken empanadas or flautas.

Storage: Keeps refrigerated in airtight jars for at least 2 weeks without losing flavor.

Preparation time: About 40 minutes

Yield: About 3 cups

RAJAS RELISH

Rajas *is the Spanish word for "slivers" or "strips"; in the Southwest, it also refers to strips of cooked chiles. The usual procedure for preparing rajas is to either grill bell peppers or chiles or blister them in hot oil, peel and seed them, and cut them neatly into strips. Either way, avoid cooking them for too long or they will become overly soft and darken: 1 minute should be sufficient. This recipe uses a fiesta of different colored chiles – red, yellow, dark green, and light green. They are all thick-fleshed, which gives the relish a satisfying texture and rich, soft flavor.*

1 red bell pepper
1 yellow bell pepper
1 poblano chile
1 New Mexico or Anaheim green chile
$\frac{1}{2}$ cup cider vinegar
$\frac{1}{2}$ cup unseasoned rice vinegar
$\frac{1}{2}$ cup sugar
2 tablespoons peeled and grated fresh ginger
2 tablespoons fresh lime juice
$\frac{1}{2}$ teaspoon salt
1 teaspoon cayenne chile powder

To prepare the rajas, roast, peel, and seed the bell peppers and chiles, and cut them into $\frac{1}{4}$-inch strips. Place the vinegars, sugar, and ginger in a stainless steel or other nonreactive saucepan, and bring to a boil. Reduce the liquid by half. Add the strips of bell pepper and chiles, and return to a boil. Reduce heat to medium and cook for 5 minutes; the peppers and chiles will release some of their juices so the mixture will have a somewhat thick consistency. Let cool, and stir in the lime juice, salt, and cayenne.

Serving suggestions: Serve cold or at room temperature with freshly shucked oysters, or warm with grilled pork or on top of grilled halibut or bass.

Storage: This relish holds its flavor and texture for up to 1 week in an airtight container.

Preparation time: About 40 minutes

Yield: About 1$\frac{1}{2}$ cups

HATCH CHILE PICCALILLI

Piccalilli is a highly seasoned vegetable relish often used in New England, it is a traditional accompaniment to baked beans. The version I remember was rather sweet, and it was made with tomatoes, onions, and sweet chiles. I loved to eat it whenever I could, and I'd sneak spoonfuls of it all the time from the refrigerator. In one of my early taste adventures, I remember once trying some piccalilli on ice cream. Fortunately, that did not become a habit!

One theory on the origin of piccalilli is that it is of Indian derivation; another is that in the early 1800s, the Shakers made batches of "pickled lily" with chopped vegetables, vinegar, and spices. It also bears a resemblance to chowchow, a Chinese relish that was introduced to California by Chinese immigrant workers in the 1940s.

1 tablespoon virgin olive oil
8 Hatch (New Mexico) green chiles, roasted, peeled, seeded, and cut into $\frac{1}{4}$-inch dice
1 red bell pepper, seeded and cut into $\frac{1}{4}$-inch dice
$\frac{1}{2}$ white onion, peeled and cut into $\frac{1}{4}$-inch dice
1 cup fresh corn kernels (cut from 1 large ear)
4 plum tomatoes, cut into $\frac{1}{4}$-inch dice
$\frac{1}{2}$ cup apple cider vinegar
$\frac{1}{4}$ cup sugar
1 teaspoon toasted dried oregano, finely ground
1 teaspoon toasted cumin, finely ground
1 teaspoon salt
2 tablespoons chopped fresh chives

In a stainless steel or other nonreactive saucepan, heat the oil and sauté the chiles, bell pepper, onion, and corn over medium heat for 5 minutes. Add the tomatoes, vinegar, sugar, oregano, cumin, and salt and cook over medium-low heat for 10 minutes, stirring occasionally. Let cool and garnish with the chives.

Serving suggestions: Serve at room temperature with barbecued dishes.

Storage: Keeps well for weeks in the refrigerator.

Variation: For a hotter relish, add 1 minced serrano chile. For notes on Hatch green chiles, see page 4. If you can't get these chiles, substitute the same number of Anaheim chiles, plus 2 jalapeños.

Preparation time: About 40 minutes

Yield: About 4 cups

GRANDAD KIFFIN'S BUMPER CROP RELISH

Eldon Kiffin, Mark Kiffin's grandfather, had a distinct knack for growing incredible tomatoes beside his house in Omaha, Nebraska. Every summer, he'd harvest a bumper crop of beefsteak tomatoes, and he grew so many that he'd give most of them away to his neighbors. He also liked to stew his tomatoes down into relishes, and this is an adaptation of his recipe.

For best results, use only the freshest vine-ripened tomatoes. Most commercial tomatoes, especially out of season, are ripened with ethylene gas and tend to be tasteless and mushy; avoid these at all costs. Adding a sprig of fresh rosemary or thyme while cooking adds a wonderful herbaceous flavor.

4 tomatoes (about 1 pound), cut in half
1 cup sun-dried tomatoes (not oil-packed)
1 cup warm water
¾ cup virgin olive oil
½ medium onion, peeled and finely minced
8 cloves roasted garlic, peeled and minced
2 tablespoons dark brown sugar
2 tablespoons sherry vinegar
2 tablespoons water
1 teaspoon salt
Sprig of fresh rosemary or thyme, optional

Preheat the oven to 350 degrees. Place the tomatoes on a baking dish and roast in the oven for 30 minutes. Remove from oven and cut into ¼-inch dice. Meanwhile, rehydrate the sun-dried tomatoes in the warm water, about 20 minutes, and drain. In a nonreactive or stainless steel saucepan, heat the olive oil and sauté the onion and garlic over medium heat until soft and translucent, about 5 minutes. Add the sugar, vinegar, water, and salt, and bring to a low simmer. Stir in both the roasted and rehydrated tomatoes and continue to cook slowly over medium heat for 20 minutes.

Serving suggestions: Serve warm or at room temperature with grilled meats and sausages.

Storage: Keeps for at least 1 week in the refrigerator.

Preparation time: About 1 hour

Yield: About 4 cups

FIVE ALLIUM RELISH

Onions, scallions, leeks, and garlic are all bulb vegetables and members of the allium family, which in turn is a branch of the lily family. All of them give off sulphur fumes when cut, and you are likely to become teary when handling them because the vapor, when combined with the natural moisture in your eyes, forms a mild sulphuric acid that acts as an irritant. Keeping these vegetables well chilled before cutting them makes the sulphur less volatile and reduces their effect on the eyes. All of the allium family members are considered strong, but when they are cooked down, they become naturally sweeter and more mellow in flavor. If you like to cook with any or all of these ingredients, this is definitely the relish for you!

¼ cup virgin olive oil
1 white onion, peeled and cut into ¼-inch slices
1 red onion, peeled and cut into ¼-inch slices
1 bunch scallions, white and green parts, cut into ⅛-inch slices
1 leek, white part only, cut into ⅛-inch slices
4 cloves garlic, cut into ⅛-inch slices
½ teaspoon sugar
½ teaspoon chile caribe
¼ teaspoon salt
½ cup sherry vinegar
1 tablespoon chopped fresh thyme leaves
¼ teaspoon freshly ground black pepper

In a nonreactive sauté pan, heat the oil and sauté the onions, scallions, leek, and garlic over medium-high heat for about 10 minutes or until golden brown. Add the sugar, chile caribe, and salt, and reduce until the mixture thickens, about 5 to 10 minutes. Add the vinegar and stir in. When the mixture thickens again, remove from heat. Stir in the thyme and pepper, and let cool.

Serving suggestions: Serve at room temperature with burgers and sausages, or use as a pizza topping.

Storage: Keeps for up to 1 week in the refrigerator.

Variation: Add a little cardamom and chopped sun-dried tomatoes, either rehydrated dried tomatoes or the kind that are packed in oil.

Preparation time: About 45 minutes

Yield: About 1 cup

MARTINI RELISH

Mark Kiffin created this recipe for his sister Diane and her husband Ric on the rooftop deck of their Manhattan apartment one steamy summer evening. The three of them discovered that this relish spread on fresh, crusty baguettes, is the perfect accompaniment for gin martinis. This recipe benefits from being prepared neatly by hand, although using a food processor will also work. Use good-quality olives and avoid the cheap pitted variety – the difference in taste is enormous.

Olives have been cultivated in the Mediterranean region for thousands of years, and are the fruit of an evergreen tree (for notes on olive oil, see page 38). They were introduced into the New World by the Spanish and now grow extensively in both North and South America. Here's an interesting piece of trivia for olive lovers: all the olive trees in South America are descended from just three trees that the Spanish planted in Peru in 1560.

1 cup black Kalamata olives, pitted
½ cup black Greek olives, pitted
1 cup green Sicilian olives, pitted
½ cup wild mushrooms, cut into ¼-inch dice
1 small carrot, peeled and cut into ⅛-inch dice
2 shallots, peeled and cut into ⅛-inch dice
2 cloves garlic, peeled and minced
½ cup virgin olive oil
¼ cup red wine vinegar
2 tablespoons finely chopped fresh basil leaves
1 tablespoon finely chopped fresh thyme leaves
2 teaspoons freshly ground black pepper

By hand, or in a food processor, finely chop the olives into ¼-inch dice (be careful they don't become mushy) and transfer to a bowl. Add the mushrooms, carrots, shallots, and garlic to the bowl with the olives, mixing well. Stir in the oil, vinegar, herbs, and black pepper. The mixture should be thick and shiny with a wonderful, sweet smell.

Serving suggestions: Serve at room temperature with fresh crusty bread and martinis, new potatoes, and rare tuna.

Storage: Keeps for weeks in the refrigerator.

Variation: Add some diced sun-dried tomatoes for an additional flavor ingredient and color contrast. Use either rehydrated sun-dried tomatoes, or the kind that are packed in oil.

Preparation time: About 30 minutes

Yield: About 4 cups

SKUNKWEED PICKLES

Epazote is a Mexican herb that is also known as wormseed, and as skunkweed, because of its pungent, resin-like aroma. It has large, spiky-edged leaves and grows prolifically, even in certain areas of the United States. Epazote is commonly cooked with black beans in Mexico and Central America. It is gradually becoming better known in the United States, but it is still more commonly available in dried form rather than fresh, which is too bad as the flavor of fresh epazote is much more pronounced. Fresh epazote makes all the difference in zipping up this variation of bread and butter pickles.

Note: Jerusalem artichokes, or sunchokes, are not in fact artichokes, but tubers related to the sunflower. They have a thin skin, and do not need to be peeled. They are in season from the fall through the spring. Asafran is a Mexican form of saffron. If you can't get it, you can substitute 1 teaspoon true saffron or ½ teaspoon turmeric.

¼ cup salt

½ cup water

½ cup crushed ice

12 small pickling cucumbers, peeled and cut into ¼-inch thick slices (about 6 cups)

2 sweet onions, or white onions, peeled and cut into ¼-inch thick slices

3 cups cider vinegar

2 cups sugar

1½ tablespoons mustard seeds

2 tablespoons coriander seeds

1 tablespoon celery seeds

2 dried chiles de árbol

1 tablespoon ground asafran

4 Jerusalem artichokes (about 8 ounces), scrubbed clean and cut into ¼-inch slices

½ cup fresh epazote leaves

In a large bowl, dissolve the salt in the water and add the ice. Add the sliced cucumbers and onions, mix thoroughly, and let sit at room temperature for 1 hour. Rinse in cold water, drain well, and set aside.

In a stainless steel or other nonreactive saucepan, bring the vinegar, sugar, seeds, chiles de árbol, and asafran to a boil, and continue to boil for 5 minutes to reduce slightly. Add the cucumbers, onions, Jerusalem artichokes, and epazote leaves, and return to a boil. Cook over high heat for 5 minutes. Remove pan from heat and let cool slightly. While still warm, divide into storage jars and seal. Keep refrigerated for at least 1 week before using.

Serving suggestions: Serve cold as hors d'oeuvres, or with burgers, sausages, and fried foods such as fish and chips.

Storage: Stays crunchy for up to 1 month in the refrigerator.

Variation: For a spicier flavor, add 1 tablespoon seeded, chopped serrano or jalapeño chile along with the cucumbers and onions.

Preparation time: About 1½ hours

Yield: About 2 quarts

SUMMER HARVEST ESCABECHE

Escabeche *is the Spanish word referring to a marinade or pickling liquid. In Mexico, it is common to find vegetables and fish or poultry dishes* en escabeche. *This recipe uses a number of garden vegetables and preserves the color and abundance of summer for the long winter months ahead. In New Mexico, gardens are at their most prolific at the end of the summer when the days are getting noticeably shorter and the nights cooler. In the high mountain valleys of the Rio Grande and Rio Chama, the first frosts usually come as early as mid-September, so it's often necessary to put up fruits and vegetables before then.*

*Don't be put off by the length of the ingredients list – this is a straightforward recipe that only takes half an hour to make. For the neatest possible presentation, take care to cut and slice the vegetables to a uniform size. For maximum color contrast, substitute 2 red jalapeño chiles for 2 of the green if they are available. Güero chiles are pale yellow chiles (*güero *is Spanish for "blond"), about 3 to 5 inches long and tapered. Other yellow chiles that can be used are the manzana and Santa Fe Grande chiles.*

Pickling Liquid:

2 cups water
2 cups cider vinegar
2 cups unseasoned rice vinegar
2 cups sugar
1 tablespoon salt
2 tablespoons coriander seeds
2 sticks cinnamon
3 whole cloves
5 allspice berries
1 teaspoon black peppercorns
1 tablespoon chile caribe
4 dried bay leaves
1 bunch fresh thyme sprigs
1 bunch fresh marjoram sprigs

Ingredients:

2 onions, peeled and cut into ¼-inch slices
12 cloves garlic (1 head), peeled
2 carrots, peeled and cut on the bias in ¼-inch slices
2 red bell peppers, seeded and cut into ½-inch thick strips
1 yellow bell pepper, seeded and cut into ½-inch thick strips
4 jalapeño chiles, with seeds, sliced into ¼-inch rings
6 serrano chiles, with seeds, sliced into ¼-inch rings
4 güero chiles, seeded and cut in half

In a large nonreactive or stainless steel saucepan, bring the pickling liquid ingredients to a boil. Add the onions, garlic, and carrots and return to a boil. Continue to boil for 5 minutes. Add the bell peppers and chiles, return to a boil, and cook for 2 minutes (do not overcook or the vegetables will be mushy rather than crunchy).

Remove pan from heat and let cool slightly. While still warm, divide into storage jars and seal. Keep refrigerated for at least 1 or 2 days before using.

Serving suggestions: Serve cold as hors d'oeuvres, or as snacks, and bar-type food.

Storage: Stays crunchy for weeks in the refrigerator.

Preparation time: About 30 minutes

Yield: About 3 quarts

ZIPPY ZUCCHINI PICKLES

As anyone who has ever grown zucchini knows, there comes a time in the middle of summer when it seems as though the squash have formed a conspiracy to overrun everything. They usually succeed for a while, and you briefly feel as though you never want to look another squash in the stamen again, let alone eat one. Of course, this phase passes, and meanwhile you've put up these pickles. Later on, after squash season, you'll wish you'd put up more because they're so darn good.

½ cup salt

1 cup water

1 cup crushed ice

6 green zucchini, cut on the bias in ½-inch slices (about 3 cups)

6 yellow zucchini, cut on the bias in ½-inch slices (about 3 cups)

2 cups water

3 cups cider vinegar

1 cup sugar

2 tablespoons salt

2 tablespoons coriander seeds

10 small whole cloves

3 allspice berries

1 bunch fresh marjoram sprigs

1 white onion, peeled and cut into ½-inch slices

4 cloves garlic, peeled

2 New Mexico or Anaheim green chiles, halved, seeded, and cut on the bias in ¼-inch slices

In a large bowl, dissolve the salt in the water and add the ice. Add the zucchini, mix thoroughly, and let sit at room temperature for 1 hour. Rinse in cold water, drain well, and set aside.

Put the water, vinegar, sugar, salt, coriander seeds, cloves, allspice, and marjoram in a stainless steel or other nonreactive saucepan and bring to a boil. Add the zucchini, onion, garlic, and chiles, return to a boil, and cook for 2 minutes. Remove pan from heat and let cool slightly. While still warm, divide into storage jars and seal. Keep refrigerated for at least 1 week before using.

Serving suggestions: Serve cold with picnic food. Good with fried chicken and slaw.

Storage: Keeps for weeks in the refrigerator.

Variation: To add a complexity of flavor, roast or smoke the chiles (see page 119). This process also makes them easier to peel. For a spicier flavor, add 2 to 3 seeded and halved serrano chiles.

Preparation time: About 1¼ hours

Yield: About 3½ quarts

FLAVORED OILS AND SALAD DRESSINGS

Flavored oils are one of the newest culinary tools to appear on the food scene, and over the last few years they have really come into vogue. They have endless uses, alone or in combination with other ingredients. Besides using them to sauté foods, you can use them to replace heavy cream-based sauces, and as marinades, salad dressings, or pasta toppings. Drizzle a little over ripe tomatoes, swirl some into soups, put some on baked potatoes or vegetables instead of butter, or use to baste food when you're grilling. If you're feeling adventurous, try a little "plate painting," using one or two colorful oils to create a border or design around the food you're serving.

There are many oils suitable for flavoring, including olive, peanut, safflower, vegetable, grapeseed, and canola oils (see below for more information on the various oils). The main requirement is that the oil be mild, and have a fresh taste and good fragrance. Once it has been flavored, the oil should be redolent of the aroma and taste of the ingredients with which it has been infused, and should never be bland. Flavored oils make great gift items, too: those that are seasoned with strong herbs, aromatic spices, and chiles, will be appreciated especially by people who are stocking a Southwestern pantry.

✣ A BRIEF GUIDE TO OILS ✣

Cooking oil is one of the most important of all the pantry items and should be thoughtfully chosen. Oils can lend a distinctive flavor and character to foods, or act as the perfect neutral medium that allows the natural flavors of other ingredients to emerge. Whether you use a strongly flavored oil or a relatively bland one depends on the effect you want. The following guide can help you in your selection. A word of caution first, though. Oils are volatile and are susceptible to evaporation and spoilage if they are stored for too long or subjected to high temperatures, so buy them in small quantities, store in a cool, dark place, out of sunlight, and use them up fairly quickly.

OLIVE OILS

✤ **Olive oil** is a basic oil for any pantry, and the one used most in this book. Olive oil comes in three main grades, reflecting the pressing process by which the oil is extracted from the ripe olives. **Extra-virgin olive oil**, the purest, best quality, and most flavorful grade, is also the most expensive. It is produced by the first, cold pressing of the olives, and is very low in acidity (less than 1 percent).

✤ **Virgin olive oil** is the product of the pressurized and heat-assisted second pressing. It has a low acidity, of less than 3 percent. The third, hot pressing produces **pure olive oil**, which is more refined but of a relatively lower quality compared to extra-virgin or virgin oil. Pure olive oil contains up to 25 percent of virgin olive oil which is added back for flavor, color, and aroma. **Light olive oil** is pure olive oil that is filtered more finely and has a lighter color and flavor as a result. It is not lighter in terms of either calories or fat.

✤ Both pure and light olive oils have a significantly higher smoking point than extra-virgin olive oil, which makes them better for frying. Because it is so strongly flavored, extra-virgin olive oil is best used for what the Italians refer to as "anointing," finishing a dish by sprinkling a few drops on the food. This same principle applies to flavored oils.

✤ The main producers of olives and olive oil are (in order of output) Spain, Italy, Greece, and North Africa. **Spanish olive oil** comes from two main growing areas: Catalonia, the area around Barcelona, which produces oil that is characterized by herbaceous tones of the Arbequina olives; and Andalusia, in southern Spain, which produces a fruity oil made principally from Manzanilla olives. My favorite olive oil from any source is made by the Vea family of Lerida in Catalonia.

✤ **Italian olive oil** is produced in four main growing areas, and each type has its own characteristics. Olive oil from Liguria, in the northwest, is light but rich, while that produced in Tuscany, in central Italy, is intense, fragrant, fruity, and peppery, and is usually dark green in color. The oil from Umbria, to the south of Tuscany, is very rich and fruity. Apulia, in southern Italy, produces more olive oil than any other region in the country. Oils from that area are typically soft, rich, full-flavored, and particularly redolent of ripe olives. Some olive oil labeled as Italian is actually imported in bulk from Spain and repackaged.

✤ **Greek olive oil** is distinctively strong and rustic. Olives are the principal agricultural crop of this country, and are mainly grown in the Kalamata region in southern Greece and on the island of Crete.

✤ **North African olive oil** is produced mainly by Tunisia, Morocco, and Algeria; Tunisia alone is the fourth largest olive growing country in the world. Almost all of the oil is exported to other Arab countries and to Italy.

✤ California's olive oil production is minimal, representing less than 0.5 percent of the world total. Most of the olives grown there are canned rather than processed into oil. Olives were first planted in California by Spanish friars, hence the name Mission olives.

✤ Olive oil is monounsaturated, which is considered beneficial in terms of cholesterol levels, and has a relatively high smoking point (especially light olive oil), compared to other oils. For the recipes in this book, we prefer to use virgin olive oil whenever olive oil is called for, except where the flavor-intense extra-virgin olive oil is specified. Never cook with extra-virgin oil, as the flavor and texture break down with heat.

✤ The color of olive oil is not an indication of quality. In general, the more yellow the oil, the riper the olives when picked. A greener olive oil is usually made from olives that are picked before they are completely ripe, which often occurs in more northerly climates to avoid the first frosts. Like red and white wines, yellow and green oils have their own distinct and often complex flavor characteristics.

✤ All olive oils are at their peak when pressed; they decline in quality progressively thereafter. Try to find extra-virgin olive oils with a vintage on their label, and consume them within two years of pressing. It is best to buy olive oils from stores with high turnover, and only buy as much at any one time as you can use within six months or so. Like all oils, olive oil should be stored in a cool, dark place, and kept well sealed.

OTHER OILS

✤ There are several neutral-flavored oils that are high in mono- and polyunsaturated fats and low in saturated fats, which yields health advantages. These include **corn oil**, **canola oil**, which is pressed from rapeseed, **safflower oil**, **cottonseed oil**, **grapeseed oil**, and **soybean oil**. These oils all have high smoking points which makes them ideal for cooking, especially frying.

✤ **Sunflower seed oil** is high in the more beneficial polyunsaturated fat, has a light, delicate flavor, but has a lower smoking point. Sunflowers are indigenous to North America and were cultivated thousands of years ago by Native Americans. **Sesame oil**, which is pressed from sesame seeds, takes two different forms. The lighter version has a mild, slightly nutty flavor, while the darker oriental style is more pronounced in flavor. It has a high smoking point which makes it a good choice for sautéing and frying, and it is also high in polyunsaturated fat. It is best bought in places where it is kept refrigerated, as sesame oil tends to turn rancid quickly. Health food stores are a good source.

✤ Among nut oils, **peanut oil** is similar to sesame oil in that it takes two different forms; a mild, relatively neutral type with a high smoking point, and an oriental version that has a much stronger flavor. It is high in mono- and polyunsaturated fats, and keeps indefinitely if stored in a cool, dark place. **Walnut oil** has a strong nutty flavor and aroma and is relatively expensive. It can turn rancid unless refrigerated, and even so, should be used within 3 or 4 months. It can be mixed with a blander oil to provide a more subtle flavor. **Hazelnut oil**, which is produced mostly in France, is also strong and nutty, and tastes and smells of roasted hazelnuts. It should be stored and used in the same way as walnut oil. **Almond oil** is pressed from sweet almonds. This French product is delicately and distinctively flavored, and quite expensive.

CHILE OIL

Since I am a confirmed chile aficionado, it is probably not too surprising that this is my favorite flavored oil and the one I use the most. It's simple to make and a good starting point if you've never made flavored oils before. One of my preferred midnight snacks is pasta tossed with basil and a little Chile Oil. I also like to use it to make mayonnaise, in soups, and on any type of salad. The combination of the spicy chile with the richness of the oil is very satisfying and easily complements so many flavors. As the recipe variations below illustrate, you can experiment with different chiles, or try adding some rosemary or basil to the oil.

2 cups grapeseed or vegetable oil
⅓ to ½ cup dried chile de árbol, cayenne, or
  habanero chile, with seeds, crushed

Place the oil in a saucepan and add the crushed dried chile. Heat very slowly until the oil is hot but not smoking. Remove the pan from the heat and let cool completely. Pour into a glass jar or bottle and seal tightly. Store in a cool, dark place for 2 weeks. Shake the jar or bottle every 2 days or so to blend the flavors.

After 2 weeks, strain the oil through a fine mesh strainer into a clean jar or bottle. Add 1 whole dried chile of the same variety for identification.

Serving suggestions: Use to sauté meats and fish, or for spicy dressings and marinades.

Storage: Keeps in a cool, dark place or in the refrigerator for up to 6 months. If refrigerated, the oil is best brought to room temperature before using.

Variations: It is generally best to use chiles that are very hot, fruity, and well-colored, and not bitter. The following are suitable: pulla, chipotle, guajillo, and tepín. You can also try adding a few cloves of peeled garlic, or a 6-inch sprig of rosemary, or 8 basil leaves after the oil has cooled.

Preparation time: About 1 hour

Yield: About 2 cups

SWEET BASIL OIL

Basil is a pungent herb that was originally native to India. It is a member of the mint family; with its aromatic bouquet of licorice and clove, it is probably the most popular of all the herbs – even children like it. You can experiment with red, purple, or variegated basil, or with the even more fragrant Thai basil, which bruises less easily.

Basil and olive oil are natural partners, and like the proverbial chicken and egg, it's difficult to know which came first! They are paired in so many ways in Mediterranean cuisines – in pesto, aïoli, and pistou, for example. You can't go wrong with this combination. In this recipe, the small amount of extra-virgin olive oil provides a more intense flavor without overpowering the basil.

1 cup fresh sweet basil leaves (1 large bunch)
12 cloves (1 head) roasted garlic, peeled
3 cups virgin olive oil
1 tablespoon extra-virgin olive oil

Place the basil in a jar or glass container large enough to hold the oil. Thread the cloves of garlic on a wooden skewer and put it in the jar (this will keep the garlic suspended in the oil). Add the olive oils, seal tightly, and store in a cool, dark place for 1 week to fully blend the flavors.

Serving suggestions: Use as you would an unflavored olive oil, for sautéing or in vinaigrettes. Sprinkle on fresh vine-ripened tomatoes or on grilled eggplant, pour over new potatoes or braised tuna, and use to baste grilled chicken, crab, scallops, and lobster.

Storage: Keeps refrigerated for up to 6 months. The oil is best brought to room temperature before using.

Preparation time: About 10 minutes

Yield: About 4 cups

TOASTED CUMIN OIL

Cumin is a building block in Southwestern and Tex-Mex cuisines, just as it is a mainstay of Middle Eastern and North African cooking. It has a woodsy, slightly smoky quality, and its aroma is reminiscent of the open range or high desert. Toasting cumin intensifies its flavor and aroma: toasted cumin smells almost like burning logs or grassland. No wonder, then, that cumin particularly complements wild game. Cumin should be used sparingly so that it can provide an important background element in a composition, yet not overpower the other flavors.

3 tablespoons cumin seed
1 teaspoon dried oregano
3 cups virgin olive oil
2 tablespoons extra-virgin olive oil

In a small sauté pan, toast the cumin and oregano over medium heat for 1 to 2 minutes, tossing occasionally. Transfer to a spice mill or coffee grinder and pulse until roughly ground. Place in a jar or glass container large enough to hold the oil. Add the olive oils, seal tightly, and store in a cool, dark place for 2 weeks to allow the flavors to fully blend. Before using, slowly strain the oil and discard the sediment.

Serving suggestions: Use for sautéing vegetables, refrying chile sauces, and brushing on breads or rolls. This oil can also be used to make a Southwestern vinaigrette.

Storage: Keeps in a cool, dark place or in the refrigerator for up to 6 months. If refrigerated, the oil is best brought to room temperature before using.

Preparation time: About 10 minutes

Yield: About 3⅓ cups

CINNAMON OIL

Cinnamon is the inner bark peeled from the shoots of the tropical laurel tree. When the bark dries, it rolls up so that it looks like a hollow stick; you can buy it in stick form or as ground cinnamon. The use of cinnamon dates back to long before the Christian era: history records that it was used by the ancient Greeks and Romans. It was used in Europe during the Renaissance to flavor out-of-the-ordinary savory dishes, and its use at that time was a sign of great affluence.

Most people associate the sweet flavor of cinnamon with desserts, but it can also be used to flavor main courses (it is especially good with grilled fish) or salad dressings. I prefer the Mexican canela, which is softer, mellower, and sweeter than regular Ceylonese cinnamon. Fresh cinnamon should have a sweet, pungent aroma and a rich coffee color; if it has little smell and a faded appearance, try another source.

2 cups grapeseed or vegetable oil
4 or 5 cinnamon sticks, crushed

Place the oil in a saucepan and add the crushed cinnamon. Heat very slowly until the oil is hot but not smoking. Remove the pan from the heat and let cool completely. Pour into a glass jar or bottle and seal tightly. Store in a cool, dark place for 2 weeks, shaking the jar or bottle every 2 days or so to blend the flavors.

After 2 weeks, strain the oil through a fine mesh strainer into a clean jar or bottle. Add 1 whole cinnamon stick for identification.

Serving suggestions: Marinate fish in it and drain it off before grilling, or brush some on the fish as you grill. Also good as a salad dressing.

Storage: Keeps in a cool, dark place or in the refrigerator for up to 6 months. If refrigerated, the oil is best brought to room temperature before using.

Preparation time: About 1 hour

Yield: About 2 cups

LEMON OIL

This is another favorite of mine – the perfume alone is wonderful, and the lemon flavor captures the essence of the sun and makes food spring to life. Try to find Meyer lemons, which are more aromatic, and take care not to include any of the bitter pith or white part. For a spicier lemon oil, use the zest of rinsed preserved lemons (a good Moroccan cookbook will tell you how to make preserved lemons).

2 cups grapeseed or vegetable oil
Zest of 4 lemons (about ¼ cup)

Place the oil and zest in a jar or glass container large enough to hold the oil. Seal tightly, and store in a cool, dark place for 1 week before using to fully blend the flavors. Shake the jar every 2 days or so to blend the flavors.

Serving suggestions: Toss it with pasta, or use it to baste grilled foods (it's especially good with seafood and veggies). You can also use it as a sauce, like drawn butter, for steamed shellfish and crudités.

Storage: Keeps in a cool, dark place or in the refrigerator for up to 6 months. If refrigerated, the oil is best brought to room temperature before using.

Variations: Add 1 teaspoon pure lemon oil extract, a commercial product made from lemon peel, available from some spice companies. You could also add one or two fresh laurel or orange leaves. Substitute grapefuit, orange, or tangerine zest for the lemon zest, or use the zest of preserved lemons.

Preparation time: About 10 minutes

Yield: About 2 cups

SALAD DRESSINGS

oo often, salad dressings lack sufficient flavor, and because of this, the tendency is to apply them with a heavy hand, drowning out the more delicate flavors of the fresh greens and vegetables or fruit in the salad. The purpose of dressings is to enhance salad ingredients and not to cover up and mask their flavors. Dressings should be used sparingly to create a light veil – after all, in the summer, it's better to dress in a light silk shirt rather than to bundle up in a heavy woolen overcoat and muffler!

Most of the dressing recipes that follow are colorful and strongly flavored, so you only need a little to dress salads and let their delicious garden flavors come through. These dressings are adaptable and can also be used to pep up rice, risottos, and grains such as quinoa, bulgur, and wheat. When used this way, they should be added late in the cooking process so the aromatic qualities of the herbs don't evaporate. In general, dressings are best made just before using.

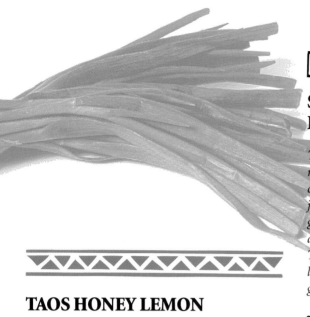

SUMMER SCALLION-LIME DRESSING

This dressing uses raw egg yolks as a base, which may raise some doubts among the skeptics. There is little cause for concern, though, as the acid from the lime juice and vinegar will inhibit harmful germs from growing. As long as the dressing is refrigerated immediately and kept chilled, there should be no problem. The freshness of the scallion and the tartness of the lime make a great combination; the two are used together in many Southwestern dressings.

2 egg yolks
¼ cup imported sherry vinegar
1 teaspoon Dijon mustard
1 teaspoon sugar
1 tablespoon fresh lime juice
½ teaspoon salt
¾ cup roughly chopped scallions, green parts only (15 to 20)
1 tablespoon fresh cilantro leaves
1 cup virgin olive oil

In a blender, blend together the egg yolks, vinegar, mustard, sugar, lime juice, and salt. With the machine still running, add the scallions and cilantro, and purée. Add the oil in a slow and steady stream until completely absorbed. Refrigerate immediately and keep chilled.

Serving suggestions: Serve chilled as a wonderful dressing for salads (especially smoked salmon salad), on avocados, as a dip for grilled vegetables or beans, or warm as a sauce for grilled fish, scallops, or chicken.

Storage: This dressing will keep covered in the refrigerator for up to 2 or 3 days.

Variation: Substitute watercress for the cilantro.

Preparation time: About 5 to 10 minutes

Yield: About 2 cups

TAOS HONEY LEMON DRESSING

Taos, which is located in northern New Mexico, is renowned for the Taos Pueblo, which is the largest existing pueblo settlement, and home to 1,500 Indians. Taos Pueblo has existed for more than 900 years, making it the oldest continuously occupied community in the United States. It is one of the best examples of Native American ecological architecture, with the buildings seeming to be a part of the land itself.

Taos is also famed for its honey. The local honey bees gather nectar from the wild mountain flowers and from the blossoms in the orchards along the Rio Grande. This gives Taos honey a delicious, unique flavor, quite different from honey made with the nectar from the more usual clover or citrus groves.

1 lemon
1 cup honey
½ cup unseasoned rice vinegar
¼ cup peanut oil
1 teaspoon pure red chile powder

Zest the lemon, being careful not to include any of the bitter white part. Finely mince the zest. Squeeze the lemon juice into a bowl, and add the zest and remaining ingredients. Combine well and chill.

Serving suggestions: Use it as a dressing for cold pasta salads or as a barbecue glaze. Brush it on breads before grilling.

Storage: Holds for up to 1 week in the refrigerator before the lemon flavor diminishes.

Preparation time: About 10 minutes

Yield: About 2 cups

JERKY DRESSING

Jerky has long been a staple item in the Native American pantry. The Plains Indians made jerky by drying buffalo and other game meats; these preserved meats helped them survive the long winter months when hunting was impossible and meat was scarce. Early hunters and trappers on the Western frontier of the United States also depended on jerky for sustenance. It remains a favorite of hikers and hunters today, not only because it makes a tasty high-protein snack, but also because it is light, easily carried, and keeps well.

It is easy to make jerky at home (you will find a recipe for it in the Coyote Cafe cookbook). You can use any low-fat meat (fats tend to turn rancid) such as beef, antelope, buffalo, or elk, and even fish can be dried into jerky. Homemade jerky has the significant advantage over commercial jerky of containing much less salt and no chemical additives. Jerky is usually eaten as snack, but it can also be used in stuffings and sauces, in scrambled eggs, or sprinkled over salads. In this recipe, it is used to add flavor to a creamy salad dressing.

6 ounces beef jerky, roughly chopped

1 cup hot water

2 tablespoons virgin olive oil

2 shallots, peeled and minced

4 cloves roasted garlic, peeled and minced

¹⁄₂ cup Mayonnaise (page 121)

¹⁄₄ cup sour cream

¹⁄₂ cup buttermilk

1 tablespoon balsamic vinegar

1 tablespoon fresh lemon juice

2 tablespoons freshly grated Asiago or Parmesan cheese

¹⁄₄ teaspoon cayenne chile powder

¹⁄₈ teaspoon salt

Rehydrate the jerky in the water for 15 minutes, drain, and mince. Meanwhile, heat the olive oil in a skillet and sauté the shallots and garlic over medium heat for 5 minutes. Transfer to a mixing bowl and let cool. Add the jerky, and combine thoroughly with the remaining ingredients. Keep refrigerated.

Serving suggestions: Serve chilled with romaine lettuce salads, or as a dip for wild mushrooms or cold beef.

Storage: Will keep refrigerated for up to 4 or 5 days.

Variation: Substitute cooked smoked bacon for the jerky.

Preparation time: About 30 minutes

Yield: About 2 cups

MINTY YOGURT DRESSING

Yogurt is very popular because of its healthful properties: it is low in saturated fat and high in vitamins, protein, and calcium. If possible, use an unpasteurized natural yogurt as it will contain the acidophilus culture, which is beneficial to the digestive system. Using a blender gives the dressing a thicker consistency, making it seem richer. Like a raita, the traditional Indian side dish that is made with yogurt, cucumber, and herbs, this dressing acts as a good cooling accompaniment for spicy food, and is especially refreshing on a hot day.

I cup plain nonfat yogurt
Zest and juice of ½ lemon
I tablespoon minced spearmint
Pinch of salt
Pinch of cayenne chile powder
2 teaspoons honey
2 tablespoons buttermilk
2 tablespoons vegetable or peanut oil

Place the yogurt, lemon zest and juice, spearmint, salt, cayenne, honey, and buttermilk in a blender, and purée. With the machine running, pour in the oil in a slow and steady stream until completely absorbed. Keep chilled.

Serving suggestions: Serve chilled with butter lettuce salads, tropical fruit salads, with baked potatoes, or rolled shoulder of lamb.

Storage: This dressing keeps for up to 5 or 6 days in the refrigerator.

Variations: If you wish, add some grated cucumber or serrano chile, or a little basil or cilantro. You can substitute purple-stemmed peppermint, which is somewhat stronger, for the green- or gray-green-stemmed spearmint.

Preparation time: About 15 minutes

Yield: About 1½ cups

CREAMY AVOCADO RANCHO DRESSING

Buttermilk has always been a staple Southwestern ingredient, and was commonly used on the ranch. Originally, buttermilk was the whey or milky substance that remained after butter was churned by hand, hence the name. It is now produced commercially by adding special cultures to low-fat or skimmed milk, which gives it a wonderful tangy, sour flavor. Despite its rich-sounding name, buttermilk actually has less fat and fewer calories than skim milk.

I clove garlic, peeled
½ cup buttermilk
½ tablespoon fresh lime juice
½ cup Crème Fraîche (page 121)
½ cup Mayonnaise (page 121)
I small avocado
¼ teaspoon cayenne chile powder
½ tablespoon minced fresh chives
½ tablespoon minced fresh parsley leaves
½ tablespoon minced fresh basil leaves
I tablespoon virgin olive oil
¼ teaspoon salt

Blanch the garlic in boiling water for 10 minutes. Drain and mince. Transfer to a blender and purée with the buttermilk and lime juice. Transfer to a medium-sized mixing bowl and fold in the crème fraîche and mayonnaise. Mix thoroughly. Cut the avocado in half, remove the pit, and scoop out the avaocado flesh with a tablespoon. Cut the avocado flesh into ½-inch dice, and add it to the bowl, along with the remaining ingredients, and stir to combine. Chill before using.

Serving suggestions: Serve chilled as a dressing for green summer salads, as a dip with hors d'oeuvres, or with smoked trout or salmon.

Storage: Use within 2 or 3 days, or the avocado will turn brown.

Preparation time: About 30 minutes

Yield: About 2 cups

MARK'S CAESAR SALAD DRESSING

The Caesar salad was created in 1926 by Alex-Caesar Cardini in Tijuana, which makes it a Southwestern invention and not an Italian one, as many people assume. Sad to say, the dressing is too often treated with insufficient respect and poorly made. A cart is wheeled out, a bowl produced, and old herbs and indifferent ingredients combined; remember, it doesn't matter how old the cart, or the bowl, or the waiter, but if the ingredients are old, the result will be one old Caesar salad! A good Caesar salad dressing should not contain too many elements, but just enough – the flavor depends on simplicity and high-quality ingredients. Use anchovies packed in olive oil, not soybean or cottonseed oil, a good imported mustard, a good-quality sherry vinegar, an aromatic, good-quality pepper such as tellicherry or lampong, and most importantly, your best extra-virgin olive oil.

Note: For longer storage, make the dressing without the egg yolks. Whisk in the appropriate number of egg yolks just before serving.

8 egg yolks
1½ cups extra-virgin olive oil
6 cloves garlic, peeled
8 to 10 anchovies packed in oil
1 tablespoon Dijon mustard
2 tablespoons fresh lemon juice
2 tablespoons sherry vinegar
Freshly ground black pepper to taste

Place the egg yolks in a large mixing bowl. In a food processor or blender, blend together the oil and garlic. Strain through a sieve into the mixing bowl, pressing down on the garlic to extract all the juice. Whisk to thoroughly combine the ingredients.

Rinse the anchovies under cold water for 30 seconds and cut finely into ⅛-inch pieces and add to the bowl, together with the mustard, lemon juice, vinegar, and pepper. Whisk to mix thoroughly.

Serving suggestions: For the classic Caesar salad, serve chilled with romaine lettuce, garlic croûtons, and freshly grated Parmesan cheese.

Storage: Will keep up to 2 days in the refrigerator. Without the eggs, the dressing base will keep for weeks.

Variation: Caesar salad dressing isn't the same without anchovies, but if you really don't like them, leave 'em out and add salt to taste.

Preparation time: About 20 minutes

Yield: About 2 cups

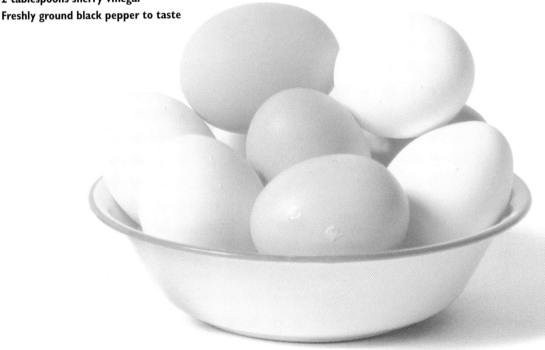

CAYENNE CREOLE RÉMOULADE

Rémoulade is a classic French sauce, believed to have originated in the Picardy region of France. It became popular in the United States with the French settlement of Louisiana, where it was adapted and used widely in the Creole and Cajun cuisines. I particularly associate rémoulade with fresh, spicy, boiled Bayou shrimp and Louisiana crawfish served in the great oyster houses off Bourbon Street in New Orleans. I am also reminded of a salad made with crawfish tails served at the Elite Cafe in San Francisco – a wonderful restaurant started by my old friend, Sam Duvall. This Creole version of the sauce gets its soul from the cayenne pepper and a healthy shot of Tabasco, that zesty, all-purpose Louisiana hot sauce. A common shortcoming of many rémoulades is a lack of scallions, so be sure to include enough; both the green and white parts should be used. And use fresh homemade mayonnaise if at all possible.

1½ cups Mayonnaise (page 121)
⅔ cup tomato purée
1 tablespoon finely ground pure chile powder
1 teaspoon cayenne chile powder
1 tablespoon Tabasco sauce
1 tablespoon whole-grain mustard
2 tablespoons fresh lemon juice
1 tablespoon chopped fresh parsley leaves
1 tablespoon chopped rinsed capers
6 to 8 scallions, green and white parts, chopped (about ½ cup)
1 anchovy packed in olive oil, rinsed and minced
1 clove garlic, peeled and minced
1 teaspoon Worcestershire sauce

Thoroughly mix all the ingredients together in a food processor or blender. The consistency should be thick, about the same as mayonnaise. Keep chilled.

Serving suggestions: Serve chilled with fried, steamed, or boiled seafood. Especially good with lobster, scallops, shrimp, and crawfish. Also use with crudités, steamed artichokes, or fries, or try it as a spread on sandwiches made with grilled chicken or fish.

Storage: Keeps refrigerated for weeks, but it will lose its flavor as time goes on.

Variation: Add 2 tablespoons chipotle chile purée (page 120) for an even spicier dressing.

Preparation time: About 30 minutes

Yield: About 3 cups

OLD-FASHIONED MOLASSES DRESSING

Molasses was the most popular (and least expensive) sweetener used in North America in the 1700s and 1800s. Originally it was part of the triangular trade that took molasses from the Caribbean to New England for processing into rum, which was then shipped to Africa in exchange for slaves, who were in turn traded for molasses in the Caribbean. Molasses is the residue that is left in the process of making sugar from sugarcane. It has a dark, syrupy taste that is associated with the ranch, and seems somehow uniquely American. Sorghum syrup, which has a similar flavor, can be used as a substitute in this recipe. My first encounter with molasses was as a traditional ingredient in the baked beans with salt pork that my grandmother used to make. She would also serve molasses at breakfast, along with homemade bread and butter.

¼ **cup dark molasses**
½ **cup honey**
¼ **cup virgin olive oil**
2 **tablespoons balsamic vinegar**
2 **tablespoons apple cider**
1 **tablespoon fresh lemon juice**
½ **teaspoon finely ground pure red chile powder**

Thoroughly combine all the ingredients in a mixing bowl, and keep refrigerated.

Serving suggestions: Warm it slightly and serve with ham, pork, or barbecued food. Try it as a dressing for a special warm salad of duck, wild mushrooms, and roasted pecans. Also good as a marinade.

Storage: Keeps for up to 1 week in the refrigerator, although it will stiffen due to the honey and molasses.

Preparation time: About 10 minutes

Yield: About 1¼ cups

BASIL BALSAMIC VINEGAR

The classic Italian balsamic vinegar is made from Trebbiano grapes. The grape juice is aged in wood barrels for several years, along with a vinegar "mother" culture. Over time, the vinegar develops a natural sweetness and an almost caramel-like flavor. The finest balsamic vinegars can cost as much as couture perfumes: for instance, a high-quality, intensely flavored balsamic vinegar that has been aged over 70 years might sell for upwards of $100 for two ounces! Balsamic vinegar was once a rarity in the United States, but moderately priced vinegars are now readily available in any well-stocked specialty or Italian market. Balsamic vinegar is stronger, smoother tasting, and has a less acidic quality compared to other vinegars, and it particularly complements the natural sweetness of fruits. One of the desserts you'll always find on a summer Italian menu is strawberries sprinkled with aged balsamic vinegar. Basil is a sweet and aromatic herb with licorice tones and is always a great match for balsamic vinegar.

2 **cups Italian balsamic vinegar**
½ **cup fresh basil leaves**
6 **cloves garlic, peeled and sliced**
1 **dried bay leaf**

Place all the ingredients in a stainless steel or other nonreactive saucepan and bring to a boil. Remove from the heat and let cool. Transfer to an airtight container and store in the refrigerator for at least 2 days. Strain the infusion, return to an airtight container, and store in the refrigerator.

Serving suggestions: Sprinkle a little over fresh fruit. This is a great ingredient to use in marinades. Combine a little with virgin olive oil or Sweet Basil Oil (page 40) to make a salad dressing.

Storage: Keeps in an airtight container in the refrigerator for up to 1 month.

Preparation time: About 10 minutes

Yield: About 2½ cups

PAINTED BEAN AND CUMIN DRESSING

I prefer warm salads, especially in the fall and winter – they are more substantial and heartier than cold salads, and they are just the right accompaniment for a light entrée. Warm salads are also a good way of using up small amounts of leftover meats. You need to do some advance preparation to make this dressing. The beans should be cooked ahead of time, and you can also rehydrate and dice the tomatoes, and toast and grind the herbs. For convenience, you can use canned beans, but rinse them under running water until the water runs clear.

2 tablespoons sun-dried tomatoes (not oil-packed)
4 ounces button mushrooms
2¹⁄₂ tablespoons plus ¹⁄₄ cup virgin olive oil
4 cloves roasted garlic, peeled and minced
2 shallots, peeled and minced
¹⁄₂ cup cooked black beans (page 110), rinsed well
¹⁄₂ cup cooked white beans (page 108), rinsed well
I tablespoon cumin seeds, toasted and finely ground
I teaspoon dried oregano, toasted and finely ground
¹⁄₄ cup water
¹⁄₄ cup Italian balsamic vinegar
2 teaspoons chopped fresh marjoram leaves
Salt to taste

Rehydrate the sun-dried tomatoes in warm water to cover, and cut into ¹⁄₂-inch dice. Clean the mushrooms and cut into ¹⁄₂-inch dice. Heat ¹⁄₂ tablespoon of the oil in a skillet and sauté the mushrooms for 5 minutes over medium heat. Meanwhile, in another sauté pan, heat 2 tablespoons of the olive oil and sauté the garlic and shallots for 1 minute over medium-high heat. Add the beans, mushrooms, and sun-dried tomatoes, and stir together. Add the cumin and oregano.

Deglaze the pan with the water and bring the mixture to a simmer. Remove pan from heat, and stir in the vinegar, remaining ¹⁄₄ cup olive oil, marjoram, and salt. Serve warm.

Serving suggestions: Perfect for wilted spinach, mustard greens, or escarole salads, served with croûtons or grilled bread on lightly warmed plates. Add a little jerky, if desired. For best presentation, arrange the salad in a large bowl, heat the dressing at the last minute, and toss the salad with the aromatic dressing at the table. To reheat the dressing, bring only to a bare simmer – do not boil. These salads can be served as an appetizer, as a side dish, or as a brunch item. The dressing is also good as a sauce with fish or chicken.

Storage: Can be refrigerated for up to 3 days, but for best results, serve immediately.

Preparation time: About 30 minutes

Yield: About 3 cups

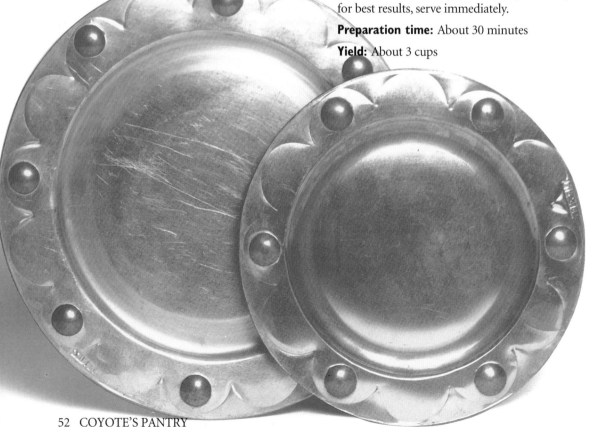

SKILLET-SEARED ARTICHOKE DRESSING

Most of the artichokes grown in the United States come from the Monterey area in northern California. The town of Castroville there bills itself as the Artichoke Capital of the World! The subtle, rich flavor of cooked artichokes belies their rather stern and fierce appearance. It is best to keep uncooked artichokes separate from other foods, and to wash the knife you cut them with before using it again; otherwise the bitterness of raw artichokes may give other ingredients an off flavor. Artichokes are in peak season during the late spring. At that time, you should be able to get the small, tightly formed baby artichokes, which are more tender and flavorful, and have no developed choke. Although fresh artichokes are best, using frozen artichoke hearts will greatly simplify the recipe. Avoid using canned artichokes, though. This recipe is best prepared ahead of time as it is rather lengthy, and the flavors develop well.

6 baby artichokes, or 2 large artichokes

2 cups water

2 tablespoons fresh lemon juice

2 tablespoons plus ½ cup virgin olive oil

½ teaspoon salt

½ cup white wine

I dried bay leaf

½ cup sherry vinegar

2 shallots, peeled and minced

I teaspoon finely ground pure red chile powder

I tablespoon finely chopped fresh basil leaves

I tablespoon finely chopped fresh thyme leaves

I tablespoon finely ground coriander seeds

I teaspoon freshly ground black pepper

To prepare the artichokes, first cut away the outer leaves until the tender inside leaves remain. Cut off the top part of the leaves to expose the white fuzzy choke inside and around the leaf ends. Scoop out the choke with a spoon, leaving the heart intact. Trim off the stem and the dark outside green parts, cut each artichoke in half, and then cut into ¼-inch dice.

Place 1 cup of the water and lemon juice in a large bowl and toss the artichoke to prevent discoloration. Drain the artichokes. In a large sauté pan, heat 2 tablespoons of the olive oil and sauté the artichokes over medium-high heat for 2 to 3 minutes. Season with ¼ teaspoon of salt and deglaze the pan with the remaining 1 cup of water and the wine. Add the bay leaf, reduce the heat to medium-low, and simmer until the liquid has almost all evaporated. Remove from the heat and set aside to cool. Discard the bay leaf.

Combine the vinegar, ½ cup olive oil, shallots, chile powder, remaining ¼ teaspoon salt, herbs, and spices in a mixing bowl, add the artichokes, and mix together thoroughly.

Serving suggestions: Serve at room temperature with other cooked vegetables, or toss with beans or olives, or use it in a tuna or Niçoise-style salad. Good with cold grilled chicken or shrimp, or as a topping for cold pasta.

Storage: The artichokes will hold their firmness and flavor in the refrigerator for up to 1 week.

Variations: Add 2 tablespoons rehydrated sun-dried tomatoes or 12 small black olives to the mixing bowl at the end.

Preparation time: About 1¼ hours

Yield: About 2 cups

SPEEDY CILANTRO DRESSING

Cilantro is such a common ingredient in Southwestern cooking, you might call it the parsley of the Southwest. It belongs to the same plant family; in fact, another name for it is Chinese parsley. (It is also known as fresh coriander, not to be confused with coriander seeds, which are quite different.) Cilantro has a pronounced, green, pungent aroma and a somewhat soapy flavor. Many people do not like it at first, but later become big fans of its distinctive, refreshing taste. A sprig in soups, salads, or grilled cheese sandwiches can make all the difference. In this recipe, cilantro is paired with lime juice, which is a natural partner.

½ cup chopped fresh cilantro leaves
¼ cup unseasoned rice vinegar
1½ tablespoons fresh lime juice
Pinch of sugar
Salt to taste
½ cup virgin olive oil

In a blender, combine the cilantro, vinegar, lime juice, sugar, and salt. With the machine still running, add the oil in a slow and steady stream until completely absorbed. Keep chilled.

Serving suggestions: Serve chilled with light summer salads garnished with avocado and mango slices, or with bean or lentil salads. Also use as a marinade to brush fish while grilling.

Storage: Best used within a day or two; it begins to lose its flavor after that.

Preparation time: About 5 minutes

Yield: About 1 cup

VELVETY GAZPACHO DRESSING

You do not need to be a rocket scientist to arrive at the stunning conclusion that most creamy dressings derive their thick texture from cream. This recipe however, uses puréed vegetables to achieve a similar texture, with the advantage that the technique produces healthier and more flavorful results. This dressing can be strained or left chunky, whichever consistency you prefer. Like its cousin, the gazpacho soup, this dressing is refreshing and cooling, and is best used on a hot summer day. For information on tomatillos, see page 3. If they are unavailable, use additional tomatoes.

5 tomatillos, husked, rinsed, and cut into ¼-inch dice
½ cup virgin olive oil
1½ tablespoons fresh lime juice
⅓ cup sherry vinegar
2 tablespoons chopped fresh cilantro leaves
½ ripe avocado, pitted, peeled, and cut into ¼-inch dice
½ red onion, peeled and cut into ⅛-inch dice
2 large plum tomatoes, seeded and cut into ¼-inch dice
½ cucumber, peeled, seeded, and cut into ⅛-inch dice
2 serrano chiles, seeded and finely minced
1 red bell pepper, seeded and cut into ⅛-inch dice
1 teaspoon salt

Place the tomatillos, oil, lime juice, vinegar, cilantro, and avocado in a blender or food processor, and purée. If you want to tone down the onion, rinse under cold water. For a smooth dressing, add the onion, tomatoes, cucumber, serranos, and red bell pepper, purée again, and season with salt. For a chunky dressing, transfer the tomatillo and avocado purée to a mixing bowl, fold the diced onion, tomatoes, cucumber, serranos, and red bell pepper into the mixture, and season with salt.

Serving suggestions: Serve with salads, especially with wild field lettuces. Try it with grilled fish.

Storage: Best used within 2 or 3 days, otherwise the avocados get too mushy.

Preparation time: About 30 minutes

Yield: About 3 cups

SMOKED TOMATO AND ROASTED SHALLOT DRESSING

Smoked or blackened tomatoes are one of the main-stays of Southwestern cuisine, and make great additions to salsas, soups, sauces, and especially red chile sauces. In this recipe, the acid of the tomatoes combines well with the creamy sweetness of the roasted shallots. Grilled vegetables take on the wonderful nuances of smoke, and the grilling process caramelizes their natural sugars, giving them great depth of flavor. Roasted shallots have more flavor than onions, and make a great side for meats. This is a rustic dressing that stands up to other strong flavors.

I pound plum tomatoes or vine-ripened garden tomatoes
4 to 6 shallots, unpeeled
I tablespoon plus ¼ cup virgin olive oil
4 cloves roasted garlic, peeled
¼ cup Italian balsamic vinegar
2 teaspoons chipotle chile purée (page 120)
½ cup fresh basil leaves
Salt to taste
Sugar to taste

Preheat the grill or broiler (for a smokier flavor, add some hardwood chips to the grill). In a mixing bowl, toss the tomatoes and shallots with 1 tablespoon of olive oil. Grill or broil the tomatoes and shallots for 10 to 15 minutes until their skins blacken slightly. Remove from heat and let cool.

Peel the shallots and place in a food processor fitted with a metal blade. Pulse together with the blackened tomatoes. Add the garlic, vinegar, chipotle purée, and basil, and pulse. With the machine still running, add the ¼ cup olive oil in a steady stream and process until emulsified. Season with salt and add sugar if the dressing tastes acidic. Keep chilled.

Serving suggestions: Serve chilled with arugula, escarole, or frisée salads and with bean or lentil salads. Also good with lamb, cold seafood, cold pasta salads, and roasted or smoked duck. Makes a great sandwich spread, too.

Storage: Holds well for up to 1 week in the refrigerator.

Variation: Fold in some sautéed wild mushrooms if desired.

Preparation time: About 25 minutes

Yield: About 2 cups

CHIVE DRESSING

The leaves of the chive plant, which is the part that is used, have a subtle flavor with a hint of garlic, but chives enhance other flavors without overpowering them as garlic would. Chives grow well on a window-sill and are easy to maintain. They are also one of the most widely available herbs in stores. They make a great garnish for soups, scrambled eggs, pastas, and salads. Chinese chives have a flat, grass-like leaf and a stronger garlic flavor, and are available in oriental markets.

2 egg yolks
3 tablespoons sherry vinegar
1 cup virgin olive oil
6 tablespoons chopped fresh chives
1½ tablespoons fresh lemon juice
¼ cup water
½ teaspoon salt
½ teaspoon freshly ground black pepper

Place the egg yolk and vinegar in a blender, and pulse. While the machine is running, add ½ cup of the oil in a slow, steady stream. Add the chives, and blend until smooth. Add the lemon juice and water to thin, then add the remaining oil in steady stream and complete the emulsification process. Season with salt and pepper. For a thicker dressing, add more oil; for a thinner consistency, add more vinegar.

Serving suggestions: Serve chilled on fresh tomatoes or cold asparagus. Also good in bean salads. Can also be used as a sauce for fish or seafood.

Storage: This dressing keeps well for 2 to 3 days, covered tightly and refrigerated.

Variation: Substitute watercress, arugula, or a little dill weed for the chives.

Preparation time: About 10 minutes

Yield: About 2 cups

SAUCES AND PASTA TOPPINGS

I am often asked to explain the difference between salsas and sauces in Southwestern cuisine. The delineation is imprecise, as they both contain similar ingredients, and both are used to accompany the same kinds of foods. There are certain differences, though. In general, salsas are composed of finely diced raw fruits or vegetables which are seasoned with vinegar or citrus juices and various spices. The individual ingredients usually keep their own form and texture. Salsas are rarely cooked, and most are served cold or at room temperature.

On the other hand, most Southwestern sauces are cooked for a period of time to combine and meld the flavors into a smooth whole. In general, it is not important for individual sauce ingredients to maintain their form. In fact, many sauces are puréed or strained. (Sometimes a chunky, roughly textured, country-style sauce works better, though, so not all sauces are puréed.) Sauces are usually served warm.

I like to use salsas to complement foods that are in their natural state and that are simply prepared; for example, tortilla chips, shellfish, eggs, and grilled meats or fish. Sauces, on the other hand, can bring a balance to more complex dishes, tying together the flavors and textures in multidimensional combinations such as wild mushroom enchiladas, or braised duck with posole.

In Southwestern cuisine, sauces tend to be intense and strong, and they are traditionally based on dried chiles. Other commonly used ingredients are roasted garlic, tomatoes, onions, and the whole range of Southwestern spices and herbs. Citrus fruits, tomatoes, and vinegar typically provide these sauces with their "high notes" and zing.

COYOTE'S RED CHILE SAUCE

When you travel through northern New Mexico in the fall, you will see ristras, *strings of ripe, red chiles, hanging up to dry against the brown adobe walls. Once dried, the chiles are stored so they can be used to make sauces like this one during the winter months. This recipe is the classic New Mexican red chile sauce, a smooth, rounded, complex accompaniment that has no sharp edges and that provides the perfect stage for a whole range of Southwestern foods, everything from tamales to* vaquero *steaks. It can also be used as a base on which to build other, more complex sauces and dishes such as red chile barbecue sauces, moles, and stews. We use this recipe at Coyote Cafe. Because it contains only one type of chile, the dried New Mexico red, the quality of the chiles is crucial to the success of the finished sauce.*

8 plum tomatoes (about 1 pound)
8 ounces (about 25) dried New Mexico red chiles
2 quarts water
1 tablespoon virgin olive oil
1 white onion, peeled and chopped
2 large cloves roasted garlic, peeled and finely chopped
1 teaspoon toasted and finely ground cumin
½ tablespoon toasted and finely ground dried oregano
1 teaspoon salt
2 tablespoons peanut oil or lard

Cut off ¼ inch of the stem end of the tomatoes. In a skillet over high heat, or under a broiler, blacken the tomatoes (about 5 minutes). Dry-roast the chiles and rehydrate them in the water (see page 120). Heat the olive oil in a skillet and sauté the onion over medium heat until browned, about 10 minutes.

Place the blackened tomatoes, rehydrated chiles, onion, garlic, cumin, oregano, and salt in a food processor or blender. If it is not bitter, add 1 cup of the chile water. Otherwise add 1 cup plain water. Purée to a fine paste, adding a little more chile water or plain water if necessary.

Heat the oil or lard in a high-sided pan until just smoking. Refry the sauce at a sizzle for 3 to 5 minutes, stirring continuously. Do not allow the sauce to become too thick; add more liquid if necessary.

Serving suggestions: Serve warm. A good accompaniment for most grilled foods. Especially good with red meats, game, such as venison, and tamales and enchiladas.

Storage: Keeps in the refrigerator for 8 to 10 days; also freezes well.

Preparation time: About 1 hour

Yield: About 4 cups

MARK'S RED CHILE SAUCE

This is my variation of the traditional red chile sauce. In this recipe, we combine several types of chile, each with its own taste characteristics and flavor dimensions (one might be fruitier, another smokier or hotter, for example), to create more complex tones and a multidimensional sauce. As a result, this is fuller, deeper, and more rounded than most other red chile sauces. The result is comparable to the depth of flavor and the variety of taste characteristics one experiences in wines composed of several grape varietals; an example of this is the new style of premium Californian red wines made from Cabernet grapes, with Merlot added for its softening quality.

Note: See the Source List (page 123) if the dried chiles called for are unavailable locally. Chipotle chiles are dried smoked jalapeños, and they can be bought canned, packed in a spicy adobo sauce. Both the chiles and sauce should be used.

8 plum tomatoes (about 1 pound)

4 ounces (about 20) dried New Mexico red chiles

2 ounces (about 5) dried ancho chiles

2 ounces (about 20) dried cascabel chiles

2 quarts water

1 tablespoon virgin olive oil

1 white onion, peeled and chopped

2 canned chipotle chiles en adobo

1 teaspoon adobo sauce

2 large cloves roasted garlic, peeled and finely chopped

1 teaspoon toasted and finely ground cumin

½ tablespoon toasted and finely ground dried oregano

1 teaspoon salt

2 tablespoons peanut oil, or lard

Cut off ¼ inch of the stem end of the tomatoes. In a skillet over high heat, or under a broiler, blacken the tomatoes (about 5 minutes). Dry-roast the chiles and rehydrate them in the water (see page 120). Heat the oil in a skillet and sauté the onion over medium heat until browned, about 10 minutes.

Place the blackened tomatoes, rehydrated chiles, onion, chipotle chiles, adobo sauce, garlic, cumin, oregano, and salt in a food processor or blender. If it is not bitter, add 1 cup of the chile water. Otherwise add 1 cup plain water. Purée to a fine paste, adding a little more chile water or plain water if necessary.

Heat the oil or lard in a high-sided pan until just smoking. Refry the sauce at a sizzle for 3 to 5 minutes, stirring continuously. Do not allow the sauce to become too thick; add more liquid if necessary.

Serving suggestions: Serve warm. A good accompaniment for most grilled foods. Especially good with red meats, game, such as venison, and tamales and enchiladas.

Storage: Keeps in the refrigerator for up to 1 week; also freezes well.

Preparation time: About 1 hour

Yield: About 4 cups

NEW MEXICO GREEN CHILE SAUCE

When you order a main course in a traditional New Mexican restaurant, you are usually asked, "Red or green?" This question refers to the color chile sauce you want (if you want both, the appropriate answer is "Christmas.") This recipe is a variation of the everyday cooked green chile sauce that is served with just about everything in New Mexico and other parts of the Southwest. It goes with all kinds of dishes, from eggs to roast beef.

Note: If you plan to serve the sauce with subtly flavored dishes (fish, for instance), do not roast the chiles, as the smoky tones of roasting may overpower the food. Instead, dip the chiles in hot oil until the skins blister. Proceed as for roasted chiles, below.

20 to 25 fresh New Mexico green chiles (about 4 pounds), or 20 to 25 Anaheim chiles with 3 or 4 jalapeños
6 cloves roasted garlic, peeled and minced
4 cups water
2 teaspoons toasted and roughly ground dried oregano
$^1/_2$ teaspoon toasted and finely ground cumin
2 teaspoons salt

Roast the chiles (see page 119) or dip them in hot oil. Put them in a bowl, cover with plastic wrap, and let them steam for 10 minutes. Peel the chiles and place them in a food processor along with the garlic, water, oregano, cumin, and salt. Chop at a medium setting: do not purée. Warm in a saucepan before serving.

Serving suggestions: Serve warm with egg dishes, enchiladas, burritos, fish, meat, and poultry.

Storage: Keeps in the refrigerator for up to 1 week; also freezes well.

Variation: Add 2 or 3 minced serrano chiles with seeds for a hotter sauce. Most Hispanics in northern New Mexico would omit the oregano as it is not a traditional ingredient in green chile sauces.

Preparation time: About 45 minutes

Yield: About 4 cups

VELARDE VALLEY APPLE CHILE SAUCE

I grew up in New England, and I remember that, in the fall, we'd drive out to the apple orchards and buy bushels of fallen apples very cheaply. Then we'd make apple pies and huge batches of applesauce. Northern New Mexico has its apple orchards, too. Driving from Santa Fe to Taos in the fall, you pass roadside stands selling rosy apples from these orchards. The community of Velarde is particularly famous for its apples, and holds an apple festival every September. The great apple orchards of New Mexico are harvested in the late summer and early fall, which is when the chiles are harvested: a perfect time to make this sauce. This recipe gives a new twist to an old favorite: it's an applesauce with a Southwestern bite.

$^1/_2$ tablespoon unsalted butter
4 green apples such as Granny Smith, (about 2 pounds), peeled, cored, and roughly chopped
4 fresh New Mexico green chiles, seeded and roughly chopped, or 2 Anaheim chiles with 1 or 2 jalapeños
2 serrano chiles with seeds, roughly chopped
$^1/_4$ cup sugar
$^1/_2$ teaspoon ground cinnamon
1 cup apple cider
1 tablespoon fresh lemon juice
$^1/_4$ teaspoon toasted and ground dried oregano
$^1/_2$ teaspoon salt

In a medium saucepan, melt the butter and sauté the apples and chiles over medium heat for 5 minutes. Stir in the sugar, cinnamon, apple cider, lemon juice, oregano, and salt. Reduce heat and simmer for 5 to 7 minutes, allowing the juices from the apples to release. Let cool slightly. Transfer to a food mill or food processor and purée.

Serving suggestions: Serve at room temperature with roasted or grilled pork, antelope, or sausages.

Storage: Will keep refrigerated for a few days.

Variation: If time permits, roast the chiles. This will give the sauce an additional depth of flavor.

Preparation time: About 45 minutes

Yield: About 2 cups

BLACKENED TOMATO AND GRILLED LEEK SAUCE

This recipe is adapted from a version my good friend Larry Forgione makes at An American Place, his landmark restaurant in New York. Blackening the tomatoes gives the sauce a smoky, earthy flavor. The leeks should be blanched enough to soften them without their falling apart during the grilling process. Buy leeks that are even in size and avoid overly large leeks in the late spring as they tend to get a tough, woody stalk towards the end of the season.

2 large leeks (about 1 pound)
16 plum tomatoes (about 2 pounds), cut in half
¼ cup virgin olive oil
½ onion, peeled and cut into ¼-inch dice
4 cloves roasted garlic, peeled and minced
1 bottle Mexican beer, such as Negra Modelo or Bohemia
1 cup water
1 teaspoon chipotle chile purée (page 120)
2 tablespoons chopped fresh parsley leaves
Salt to taste

Preheat the grill or broiler. Cut most of the green parts off the leeks, but leave the roots on as this will help hold the leeks together while they cook. Cut the leeks in half lengthwise and blanch the leeks in boiling salted water for 1 minute. Drain, and plunge into ice water. Grill the tomatoes and leeks until grill marks begin to show, or place them on a rack and broil them about 5 minutes. Remove, let cool, quarter the tomatoes, and cut the leeks into 1-inch slices, discarding the root ends.

In a pan, heat the olive oil, and sauté the onion and garlic over medium-high heat for 10 minutes, until brown. Deglaze the pan with the beer and reduce liquid by half. Add the water and continue to reduce until the sauce thickens. Add the chipotle purée, parsley, and salt, and stir in. Immediately before serving, add the reserved, chopped tomatoes and leeks.

Serving suggestions: Serve warm with grilled fish such as bass or halibut, or with clams, or red meats. To use for a pasta topping, add some chopped smoked duck or ham. Also good as a pizza topping.

Storage: Best served at once, but will keep refrigerated for up to 2 days.

Variations: You can substitute 8 ounces of scallions for the leeks. Use a full-flavored American ale instead of the Mexican beer; for example, Anchor Steam, Samuel Adams, or Sierra Nevada beer.

Preparation time: About 40 minutes

Yield: About 3 cups

SMOKY TOMATO SAUCE

Store-bought tomato sauces usually consist of taste-less tomatoes cooked with plenty of sugar and indif-ferent flavorings. They tend to be generic and you can only tell the difference between them by the labels. If you like a tomato sauce with some character, you'll find it well worth the effort to make your own. The smoky flavor of this sauce comes from both the black-ened tomatoes and the chipotle chiles. It provides the sauce with an extra dimension that complements and blends well with other flavors. If possible, use whole canned chipotle chiles packed in a spicy adobo sauce so you can use both chiles and sauce (see Source List, page 123).

8 plum tomatoes (about 1 pound)
4 cloves roasted garlic, peeled and roughly chopped
4 chipotle chiles en adobo, roughly chopped
Adobo sauce (add enough to the chipotles to make
    ¼ cup)
¼ cup loosely packed fresh cilantro leaves
1 tablespoon fresh lime juice
⅛ teaspoon salt

On a rack over a flame on the stovetop, in a cast-iron skillet, or on a grill, blacken the tomatoes until the skin blisters, about 5 minutes. Roughly chop the blackened tomatoes and transfer to a blender. Add the garlic, chipotles, cilantro, lime juice, and salt. Purée, adding a little water if necessary. Transfer to a saucepan and warm gently.

Serving suggestions: This sweet and spicy sauce is best served warm. It goes well with grilled meats, crab, and chiles rellenos. It can also be used as a base for soups and stews.

Storage: Will keep refrigerated for at least 3 or 4 days.

Variation: Add pickled jalapeños for additional heat, or some eggplant for a different flavor tone.

Preparation time: About 20 minutes

Yield: About 2 cups

FRESH FIG AND MUSCAT WINE SAUCE

Muscat grapes are my very favorite variety – they have an incredible, intoxicating perfume and a deli-ciously sweet, musky flavor. The sparkling Italian muscat wine made from these grapes is wonderfully intense and spicy. Muscats turn a deep yellow, almost amber color when they are fully ripe. Seeing them in stores during the harvest season is one of the sure har-bingers of fall.

Figs were a popular fruit in the Mediterranean re-gion at least 5,000 years ago and grew in the Hang-ing Gardens of Babylon. They were introduced to the Southwest by the Spanish settlers. Most of the figs grown in the United States come from California; they are in season there from June to October. Use the ripest figs you can find. The darker the figs, the darker the sauce will be.

1 tablespoon virgin olive oil
2 shallots, peeled and minced
10 fresh, very ripe figs, roughly chopped
1 cup chicken stock, preferably homemade
1 teaspoon finely minced fresh thyme leaves
1 tablespoon fresh lemon juice
1 cup muscat wine, such as Beaumes de Venise

In a saucepan, heat the olive oil and sauté the shal-lots and figs over low heat for 5 minutes. Add the stock, increase heat to medium, and bring to a sim-mer. Add the thyme, lemon juice, and muscat wine. Return to a simmer and remove from heat. Transfer to a blender and purée.

Serving suggestions: Serve warm with roasted duck, quail, or other dark-meated game birds. Add some smoked chicken or quail meat to it to make a pasta sauce. Use it as a glaze for grilling poultry or game birds.

Storage: Keeps for 2 or 3 days in the refrigerator; refresh with a little muscat wine if necessary.

Preparation time: About 30 minutes

Yield: About 3 cups

ANCHO SUN-DRIED CHERRY BARBECUE SAUCE

Western barbecue sauces tend to be fruitier and sweeter in style than the smokier, hotter Texas barbecue sauces or the more vinegary North Carolina-style versions. In this barbecue sauce, the intense fruit flavor of the sun-dried cherries perfectly complements the sweetness and fruity taste tones of the ancho chiles. The ancho has a deep, dark, rich red hue when held up to light, and looks like dried fruit leather. When you use naturally dried ripe fruit, you don't need to add as much sugar to the recipe as you would otherwise. Sun-dried cherries are available from specialty or health food stores or from Coyote Cafe's General Store (see Source List on page 123).

1 cup unseasoned rice vinegar
1 cup cider vinegar
¼ teaspoon ground cloves
¼ teaspoon ground allspice
½ teaspoon ground coriander
2 tablespoons virgin olive oil
¼ onion, peeled and cut into ½-inch dice
2 cloves roasted garlic, peeled and minced
½ cup brown sugar
2 tablespoons dark molasses
6 ounces sun-dried cherries
2 cups ancho chile purée (page 120)
1 14-ounce bottle ketchup
1 cup water
Salt to taste
2 tablespoons peanut oil

In a saucepan, combine the vinegars, cloves, allspice, and coriander, and bring to a boil. Reduce the liquid by half over medium heat, about 10 minutes, strain, and set aside.

In a large skillet or pan, heat the olive oil and sauté the onion and garlic over medium heat until lightly brown, about 8 minutes. Add the brown sugar and molasses, and stir until dissolved. Add the reserved vinegar reduction, deglaze the pan, and reduce slightly. Stir in the cherries, ancho chile purée, ketchup, and water. Simmer slowly for about 20 minutes. Season with salt, transfer to a blender, and purée.

Add the peanut oil to a high-sided pan and heat until just smoking. Strain the puréed sauce into the pan and refry at a sizzle for 2 to 3 minutes, stirring continuously. Do not allow the sauce to become too thick; add a little more water if necessary.

Serving suggestions: Serve warm with ribs, game birds, such as duck or quail, venison, or sausages.

Storage: Keeps in the refrigerator for 7 to 10 days.

Variation: Substitute 1 pound pitted fresh cherries for the dried, and increase the sugar to ¾ cup.

Preparation time: About 1 hour

Yield: About 3 cups

ZAPOTEC MOLE

Moles are probably the most complicated of all the Latin American sauces. Typically, a mole will contain many different ingredients, quite a few of which will require advance preparation. The ingredients are then blended and cooked together to create a sauce of intriguing complexity. Most people think that moles are chocolate sauces, but this is not true. Mole is a Nahuatl word that simply means "mixture," and the mixture need not include chocolate. Of the three mole sauces given here, only this one contains chocolate.

This particular mole is our version of the traditional mole rojo or red mole. It is made with dried ancho, mulato, and negro (pasilla) chiles. Together, these three chiles form the "holy trinity" of chiles used in the classic red and black mole sauces. The mole also contains Ibarra chocolate, a dark Mexican chocolate that is made with cacao, cinnamon, sugar, and ground almonds.

The Oaxaca region is famous for its moles. This is also where the pre-Aztec Zapotec civilization was centered. The Zapotecs almost certainly used different varieties of chiles, seeds, and vegetables, as well as chocolate and vanilla for flavoring. It is likely that they created the precursors of modern-day mole sauces such as this one.

10 dried ancho chiles (about 4 ounces)

8 dried mulato chiles (about 4 ounces)

6 dried chiles negro (pasillas) (about 4 ounces)

2 quarts water

½ cup raisins, or dried plums, or dried cherries

4 tomatillos, husked and rinsed

5 plum tomatoes

⅓ cup pumpkin seeds

½ cup almonds, unskinned

1 tablespoon peanut oil

2 6-inch corn tortillas, dried in the oven and cut into 1-inch strips

6 cloves roasted garlic, peeled

2 cups water

4 teaspoons ground canela, or 2 teaspoons ground cinnamon

4 whole cloves, ground

½ teaspoon freshly ground black pepper

6 allspice berries, ground

1 teaspoon salt

3 ounces Mexican Ibarra chocolate plus 2 ounces unsweetened chocolate, or 6 ounces unsweetened chocolate

3 tablespoons peanut oil

Rehydrate the chiles in the 2 quarts of water (page 120). Soak the raisins in enough warm water to cover for about 20 minutes, until soft. Place the tomatillos and tomatoes in a skillet or under a broiler and blacken, about 5 minutes. Dry-roast the pumpkin seeds in a sauté pan for about 5 minutes until they have finished popping; be careful not to let them burn. In a skillet, sauté the almonds in the peanut oil over medium-low heat until browned.

Place the tomatillos, tomatoes, pumpkin seeds, almonds, and tortilla strips in a food processor or blender, and purée. Add the rehydrated chiles, raisins, garlic, water, spices, and salt, and purée together. Transfer to a saucepan and cook for 30 to 40 minutes. Strain through a sieve.

Heat the peanut oil in a high-sided pan or skillet until almost smoking. Add the sauce and fry over medium heat for 10 to 15 minutes, stirring constantly. Meanwhile, melt the chocolate in a double boiler. Blend it into the sauce at the last minute. Do not allow the sauce to get too thick; add more water if necessary.

Serving suggestions: This sauce is excellent with rich, deeply flavored dishes. Especially good with poultry, especially duck or turkey. Serve warm, but not hot.

Storage: Keeps in the refrigerator for up to 1 week.

Preparation time: About 1½ hours

Yield: About 5 cups

MOLE AMARILLO

When we opened Red Sage restaurant in Washington, D.C. in early 1992, one of the most popular dishes on the inaugural menu was rare seared tuna, served with Mole Amarillo. *It is an elegant sauce – one of my favorites – and a good example of a traditional sauce that is perfectly suited to modern Southwestern cuisine. It has great flavor and color (mole amarillo means "yellow mole"). To keep the bell peppers bright yellow, they should be blistered in hot oil, not roasted. Take care not to let the sauce get too thick, and don't cook it too much or it will lose some of its aromatic qualities. Taste the güero chiles, as sometimes they have more than a little heat, and adjust the amount accordingly.*

1 tablespoon unsalted butter
1 onion, peeled and cut into ½-inch dice
15 güero chiles (about 8 ounces), halved and ¾ of the seeds removed
3 yellow bell peppers, blistered in hot oil, peeled, seeded, and quartered
8 tomatillos, husked and rinsed
3 cloves roasted garlic, peeled
½ teaspoon ground cinnamon
1 teaspoon sugar
Pinch of ground allspice
Salt to taste
2 tablespoons peanut oil

In a large, thick-bottomed pan or skillet, melt the butter and sauté the onion until soft but not caramelized. Add the chiles and bell peppers, and cook over low heat until soft, about 30 minutes.

Blanch the tomatillos in boiling water for 15 seconds, and then roughly chop. Transfer to a food processor or blender with the sautéed onions, chiles, and bell peppers. Add the garlic, cinnamon, sugar, allspice, and salt. Purée, adding a little water if necessary.

Heat the peanut oil in a high-sided pan or skillet until almost smoking. Add the sauce and fry over medium heat for 5 to 7 minutes, stirring constantly. Do not allow the sauce to get too thick; add more water if necessary. Strain the sauce through a sieve.

Serving suggestions: Serve warm, but not hot. The spicy fruit and citrus tones of this sauce go well with seafood, especially tuna and scallops, and grilled chicken.

Storage: Keeps in the refrigerator for up to 5 days.

Variations: Add 1 apple or pear: purée it in the food processor or blender before adding the tomatillos. Instead of the güeros, you can substitute 2 yellow Scotch bonnet chiles with the seeds removed and add 2 more yellow bell peppers.

Preparation time: About 1½ hours

Yield: About 2 cups

HOJA SANTA MOLE VERDE

Hoja santa *(also known as* yerba santa *or* hierba santa*) is commonly used in Mexican cooking, especially with steamed fish. This herb has a large, heart-shaped green leaf, and a wonderful sassafras or root-beer flavor and an aromatic quality that brings foods alive. It grows in subtropical regions, including southern Texas and many areas in Mexico and Central America. It is becoming increasingly popular in the United States, but is still difficult to find outside the Southwest (see page 123 for sources). If it is unavailable, use fennel tops instead.*

This is a light, tasty, and delicate sauce that originated in the Oaxaca region of Mexico. It should be cooked quickly to keep its flavors fresh, as well as to preserve its perfume and bright green color. In Spanish, verde *means "green," and this sauce is aptly named.*

6 tomatillos, husked and rinsed

I cup water

6 romaine lettuce leaves, julienned

$^1\!/_2$ cup fresh cilantro leaves

6 poblano chiles, roasted, peeled, seeded, and roughly chopped

I teaspoon coriander seeds, toasted and finely ground

2 hoja santa leaves

$^1\!/_2$ teaspoon salt

I 6-inch corn tortilla, dried in the oven and roughly chopped

2 tablespoons chopped fresh epazote leaves (optional)

2 tablespoons peanut oil

Dry-roast the tomatillos in a skillet or under a broiler for 4 to 5 minutes. Transfer to a food processor or blender and add the water, romaine, cilantro, poblanos, coriander, *hoja santa*, salt, tortilla strips, and epazote, and purée.

Heat the peanut oil in a high-sided pan until just smoking. Refry the sauce at a sizzle for 3 to 5 minutes, stirring continuously. Strain the sauce and keep warm.

Serving suggestions: Serve warm, but not hot, with seafood, poultry, and pork.

Storage: Best used the same day.

Preparation time: About 1 hour

Yield: About 4 cups

PASTA TOPPINGS

When you think of pasta sauces, you usually associate them with olive oil, butter, cream, or tomatoes. The recipes in this chapter, however, are variations based on Southwestern flavors. They are easy to make and economical, and most can be prepared ahead of time.

A common oversight in preparing pasta dishes is to mismatch the sauce with the pasta itself. The heavier the sauce, the more substantial the pasta should be to hold it. Chunky, hearty sauces should not be served with thin, fragile pasta. Sauces that are more liquid should be served with pasta shells or some other pasta with hollow areas to hold the sauce. The amount of sauce relative to the pasta is also important; ideally, the sauce should coat the pasta, and no more. The sauce and pasta should be integrated, with neither one dominating the other.

Because there are so many kinds of pasta available, it's a natural choice for quick, simple meals. Believe it or not, there are even some Southwestern-flavored pastas on the market now. For a change, try a pasta flavored with chiles, cilantro, or blue corn, and match it with one of the recipes in this chapter.

ROASTED GARLIC SAUCE

Garlic is believed to have originated in Central Asia, although there are several different theories on the subject. Its name is derived from the Old English words for "spear" (gar) and "leek" (leac).

This sauce depends on the quality of the garlic used; buy the freshest you can find, with firm bulbs, tight skin, and no sign of any sprouting. The red or purple-tinged garlic grown in Gilroy, California (the garlic capital of the world) comes into season during the summer and is sweeter than regular garlic. Roasting garlic intensifies its mellower tones and reduces its sharp edges.

2 heads roasted garlic (about 24 cloves)

2 tablespoons virgin olive oil

2 tablespoons unsalted butter

2 shallots, peeled and cut into ⅛-inch slices

1 cup heavy cream

1 cup vegetable stock or chicken stock

½ cup dry Marsala, or additional vegetable or chicken stock

½ tablespoon chopped fresh thyme leaves

1 teaspoon salt

½ teaspoon freshly ground black pepper

Peel and mince the garlic. In a saucepan, heat the olive oil with the butter, and sauté the shallots and garlic over medium heat for 5 minutes. Add the cream and stock, bring to a boil, reduce heat, and simmer for 10 minutes. Add the Marsala and simmer for 5 minutes longer. Add the thyme and season with salt and pepper. Transfer to a food processor and purée. Warm in a saucepan.

Serving suggestions: Serve warm with spaghetti, linguine, fettuccine, or raviolis.

Storage: Keeps for up to 3 or 4 days in the refrigerator.

Variation: Add ¼ cup julienned oil-packed sun-dried tomatoes when you warm the sauce.

Preparation time: About 45 minutes

Yield: About 2 cups

COONRIDGE GOAT CHEESE SAUCE

Goats, horses, pigs, and cattle were introduced to the New World by the Spanish. They were raised to provide meat, milk, cheese, and hides, and they have remained an important part of the Hispanic farming tradition. Goat meat (cabrito) is often served at celebrations such as weddings and fiestas, and on holidays, Easter in particular.

Goats have adapted very well to the semi-arid regions and high mountain grasslands of New Mexico. At Coyote Cafe, we use a wonderful goat cheese that comes from Coonridge, in southern New Mexico. Goat cheese has a tangy taste that stands up well to the stronger Southwestern flavors.

4 ounces apple- or hickory-smoked bacon, cut into ⅛- inch dice

½ onion, cut into ¼-inch dice

1 poblano chile, roasted, peeled, seeded, and cut into ¼-inch dice

½ cup chicken stock, preferably homemade, or water

2 ounces fresh or aged goat cheese

½ cup heavy cream

1 teaspoon chopped fresh thyme leaves

Salt to taste

In a sauté pan over medium heat, fry the bacon until half-cooked, about 10 minutes. Add the onion and roasted poblano, and sauté in the rendered bacon fat for about 5 minutes, until the bacon is fully cooked. Add the stock or water, and stir in the goat cheese. Increase the heat to medium-high and stir in the cream. Cook briefly to warm through; the sauce should be thick and emulsified. Remove from heat, add the thyme, and season to taste with salt.

Serving suggestions: Serve warm tossed with tortellini, fettuccine, or in lasagne. Excellent with chicken raviolis.

Storage: The sauce is best used immediately and should not be stored for longer than 1 day.

Preparation time: About 20 minutes

Yield: About 2 cups

PLATINUM LADY SAUCE

Corn was probably the most important food to the Native Americans of the Southwest, for whom it held great cultural and religious significance as well as dietary value. Like the inhabitants of pre-Columbian Mesoamerica, Native Americans have long revered corn as a gift from the ancestors for sustaining mankind. Ceremonies are still held where prayers are offered to the Corn Mother spirit.

Platinum Lady is a strain of very sweet, tender, white corn that is particularly well suited to the altitude and short growing season of the high-desert Southwest. You can substitute another type of sweet corn, such as Silver Queen, which is available on both the West Coast and the East Coast. Yellow corn can be substituted, but white corn is sweeter, and when it comes to corn, the sweeter the better.

2 ears fresh white corn

I tablespoon unsalted butter

¼ medium white onion, peeled and cut into ¼-inch dice

I teaspoon peeled and grated fresh ginger

I teaspoon chopped fresh thyme leaves

½ teaspoon salt

2 tablespoons white wine

I teaspoon sugar

I cup heavy cream

I tablespoon sherry vinegar

Cut the kernels off the cobs, and scrape the cobs with the back of the knife to squeeze out as much of the corn milk as possible. In a medium saucepan, melt the butter and sauté the onion over medium heat for 5 minutes. Add the ginger, thyme, salt, and white wine, and bring to a simmer. Stir in the corn and sugar, and return to a simmer. Add the cream, and barely simmer for 10 minutes longer or until the corn is soft. Do not allow the mixture to boil.

Transfer to a food processor or blender, and purée. Strain the sauce through a sieve, pushing down with the back of a spoon to extract as much liquid as possible. Stir in the sherry vinegar. Warm the sauce in a saucepan.

Serving suggestion: Serve warm with tortellini, linguine, or conchiglie (shells), or as a sauce with empanadas or quesadillas.

Storage: Keeps refrigerated for up to 3 or 4 days.

Preparation time: About 40 minutes

Yield: About 2½ cups

ABIQUIU TOMATO BASIL SAUCE

Abiquiu is about an hour's drive north of Santa Fe, and is most famous for having once been the home of the renowned artist Georgia O'Keeffe. One of her best-known paintings is of the beautiful red cliffs that are a striking feature of the area.

The Rio Chama runs through Abiquiu, which makes it an excellent growing region. It is here that my friend Elizabeth Berry has a spectacular ranch with a large garden. The tomatoes she grows are the best I have ever tasted, and she delivers them to Coyote Cafe just hours off the vine. Squash blossoms are another of her specialties. The first blossoms of the year always mark the beginning of the summer harvest. They are so popular, we get calls from people in the early summer who want to know if the blossoms are on the menu yet! We fry them, and serve them with this sauce.

8 plum tomatoes
1 tablespoon chopped fresh basil leaves
¼ cup virgin olive oil
1½ tablespoons sherry vinegar, or Italian balsamic vinegar
½ teaspoon salt
½ teaspoon freshly ground black pepper

Core the tomatoes and cut them in half. Gently squeeze the tomatoes to press out the juice and seeds. Place the tomatoes in a food processor fitted with a steel blade, and finely chop together with the basil. Transfer to a saucepan, stir in the olive oil and vinegar, season with salt and pepper, and warm gently.

Serving suggestions: Serve warm with pasta such as penne or ruoti (wagon wheels), stuffed deep-fried squash blossoms, or as an accompaniment for grilled fish, shrimp, poultry, or vegetables.

Storage: For best flavor and quality, prepare and use the same day.

Variation: For a heartier, smokier, and more complex flavor, roast and blacken the tomatoes (see page 120).

Preparation time: About 20 minutes

Yield: About 1½ cups

RANCHO RED BELL PEPPER SAUCE

Bell peppers are not really peppers at all; they are actually a type of chile. The word pepper *is a misnomer originated by Columbus when he discovered some small, round, red chiles in the New World and believed they were unripe black pepper berries. In part, this was wishful thinking, as black pepper was highly prized in Europe and was worth its weight in silver. The name has unfortunately and confusingly stuck ever since. Bell peppers are the mildest of all the chiles.*

2 red bell peppers
4 teaspoons plus ½ cup virgin olive oil
1 white onion, roughly chopped
2 cloves garlic, minced
2 tablespoons Italian balsamic vinegar
½ cup water
2 heaping teaspoons chopped fresh basil leaves
½ tablespoon finely ground pure red chile powder
1 tablespoon Tabasco sauce
¾ teaspoon salt

Roast, peel, seed, and roughly chop the bell peppers. In a saucepan, heat 4 teaspoons of the olive oil and sauté the onions over medium-high heat for about 10 minutes until brown. Transfer to a food processor or blender and add the bell peppers, garlic, vinegar, water, basil, chile powder, and Tabasco sauce, and pulse to mix thoroughly. With the machine still running, drizzle in the remaining ½ cup olive oil and continue to blend until completely emulsified. Season with salt. Transfer to a saucepan and warm gently.

Serving suggestions: Serve warm with fettuccine, linguine, spaghettini, or raviolis, or use as a vinaigrette or marinade.

Storage: Keeps for 3 to 4 days in the refrigerator.

Preparation time: About 30 minutes

Yield: About 2½ cups

GRILLED VEGETABLE TOPPING

I remember, from my childhood, backyard grilling and barbecued hot dogs, burgers, chicken, and steaks, but I don't recall ever seeing or eating grilled vegetables. They have become much more popular in recent years, and in today's health-conscious food market, many restaurants now offer grilled vegetable entrées. My friend Stephan Pyles, who has long pioneered modern Texan and Southwestern cuisine in Dallas, has probably done the most to popularize their appearance on menus across the country. An assortment of different colored grilled vegetables can make an easy, quick pasta dressing or a wonderful cold pasta salad, especially to accompany a main course of tuna or meat. Use a pasta with more mass, such as the tubular penne or the spiral fusilli, rather than a flat, fragile type, so it can carry the topping. Prepare this dish only when you can get the very freshest vegetables and wild mushrooms possible.

Vegetables:

2 New Mexico green, Anaheim, or poblano chiles, seeded and halved

4 plum tomatoes

2 Japanese eggplants

1 red bell pepper, halved and seeded

1 zucchini

1 yellow squash

1 red onion, peeled

1 ounce wild mushrooms, such as shiitakes or oyster mushrooms, or a combination

Other Ingredients:

½ cup virgin olive oil

2 tablespoons finely ground pure red chile powder

1 tablespoon chopped fresh marjoram leaves

½ tablespoon chopped fresh thyme leaves

¼ cup Italian balsamic vinegar

½ cup chopped fresh basil leaves

½ teaspoon salt

Grated Parmesan or Asiago cheese, or crumbled goat cheese (optional)

Prepare the grill. Cut the vegetables and mushrooms into large attractive shapes; for example, the chiles should be cut into ¼-inch strips, the tomatoes can be cut in half, and the squash into oblongs. Place the vegetables and mushrooms in a large mixing bowl and toss with ¼ cup olive oil, chile powder, and chopped marjoram and thyme. Transfer to a rack and grill until lightly browned.

Meanwhile, combine the balsamic vinegar and basil in a bowl and whisk in the remaining ¼ cup olive oil until emulsified. Drizzle the vinaigrette over the grilled vegetables, sprinkle with salt, and top with the grated cheese if desired.

Serving suggestions: Serve warm tossed with pasta such as penne or ziti, or use it in lasagne. Good in cold pasta salads. The vegetables can be served on their own as an appetizer, in which case you could omit the vinaigrette and top them with Blackened Tomato and Grilled Leek Sauce (page 65) or the Rancho Red Bell Pepper Sauce (above) instead.

Storage: For best flavor and quality, prepare and use the same day.

Variation: Add a little Sweet Basil Oil or Lemon Oil (pages 40 or 42) for an additional flavor tone.

Preparation time: About 20 minutes

Yield: About 1½ cups

GRILLING RUBS, MARINADES, AND GLAZES

In Southwestern cuisine, spices and seasonings are used to add layers of expression to ordinary ingredients. Just as an artist builds on a canvas, or a musician on a musical scale, the Southwestern chef embellishes foods with complementary or contrasting flavors. When it comes to preparing food for the grill, the simplest way to do this is to use rubs, marinades, and glazes.

Rubs and marinades have long been used to flavor and tenderize meat, and to preserve foods from spoilage or contamination. (The combination of acid and spices creates an unfavorable medium for harmful microorganisms to grow, thus assisting in the preserving process.) The modern cook should use rubs and marinades strictly to add character to the food, however, and try to select a combination of seasonings that will suit the food that is being cooked. A marinade for venison should contain herbs and spices to match the subtle, herbaceous tones of the meat, while poultry calls for fruitier tones. Bland foods undergo a transformation when they are seasoned with a zesty marinade or rub.

Rubs, which are nothing more than dry marinades, are ideal for flavoring meats or fish that will be cooked to just rare; a crunchy outer crust is created, without the flavors contained in the crust penetrating the meat too far. Avoid cooking rubs over too high a temperature, as the spices might scorch and give a bitter taste.

Rubs contain salt and spices, so care must be taken since this combination can extract some of the natural juices from the cuts of meat to which they are added. Although rubs can be applied up to 24 hours ahead of time, in general it makes sense not to leave them on too long, especially in the case of fish.

In Southwestern cooking especially, marinades have historically served the practical purpose of keeping meats moist while they were cooked over an open fire. They are also an excellent means of preparing large or relatively tough and less expensive cuts of meat that are best cooked slowly. The typical marinade will contain natural acids such as citrus and fruit juice, wine, or vinegar which penetrate the meat and tenderize it. Don't marinate foods too long, however, or the acids may actually "cook" them, rather like ceviches.

Glazes add a wonderful flavored crust to the outside of meats or vegetables, and they should generally be applied in the last few minutes of cooking, so the natural sugars don't caramelize and burn. Meats that need glazes for a longer cooking period—ham, for instance—should be cooked far enough away from the fire, or in a low oven.

Marinades can sometimes be used as glazes, too. However, if too much of the meat juices or blood are left in the marinade, the glaze will taste bitter. Another point to remember is that if too much oil is contained in the marinade, it is likely to cause the grill to flare up.

Most rubs, marinades, and glazes can be made with ingredients straight out of the pantry, and most will keep for a week or more in the refrigerator.

ANCHO CHILE BUTTER RUB

Ancho chiles are dried poblano chiles. They are the sweetest and the broadest of any dried chile (in Spanish, ancho means "wide"). They are brick-red to dark mahogany in color, heart-shaped, and wrinkled, and have a medium-thick flesh. The more pliable and more red-fleshed the ancho, the fresher and fruitier it is likely to be. Most people associate dried chiles with heat rather than flavor, but the ancho is not particularly hot. It is a good example of the range of flavors that chiles can contain: the fruity and slightly smoky tones of the ancho include hints of raisin, prune, licorice, coffee, and tobacco. If you are not used to cooking with chiles, the ancho is a good one to start with. This rub will be an attractive rosy color.

4 dried ancho chiles
1 pound unsalted butter, at room temperature
1 tablespoon brown sugar
$\frac{1}{2}$ teaspoon finely ground allspice berries
Zest of 1 orange, finely minced (1$\frac{1}{2}$ tablespoons)
1 teaspoon pure red chile powder
$\frac{1}{2}$ teaspoon salt

Break the chiles up into small pieces and rehydrate (page 120). Drain the rehydrated chiles, reserving some of the water. Purée in a blender, adding a little chile water if necessary. (If the chile water is bitter, use plain water.) The purée should be very thick. Strain the purée and let cool.

In a food processor fitted with a plastic blade, in a mixer fitted with a paddle attachment, or in a mixing bowl, thoroughly combine the chile purée, butter, sugar, allspice, orange zest, chile powder, and salt.

Serving suggestion: Bring to room temperature to soften and rub on meats before grilling.

Storage: Keeps in the refrigerator for weeks, and freezes well.

Preparation time: About 30 minutes

Yield: About 2$\frac{1}{2}$ cups

PICANTE DRIED RED CHILE RUB

Rubs, which are really dry marinades, enhance the flavors and textures of meats. Their flavorful crusts can make sauces unnecessary, and as the meat can be cooked dry, they also make cooking fats and oils unnecessary. Like marinades, rubs can be applied for a long period of time (up to 24 hours) in the case of large cuts of meat such as beef fillets or a boned-out leg of lamb, but use them for a short time or at the last minute in the case of more delicate ingredients such as fish, so the natural sugars and flavors are not overwhelmed.

2 tablespoons chile caribe
1 tablespoon dried oregano
$\frac{3}{4}$ cup pure red chile powder
1 tablespoon sugar
1 teaspoon salt

Place the chile caribe and oregano in a dry skillet and toast over medium heat for 2 minutes until fragrant. Transfer to a spice grinder and pulse until smooth. Place in a bowl and combine thoroughly with the chile powder, sugar, and salt.

Serving suggestion: Rub on meats or fish before grilling to give a spicy crust.

Storage: Keeps well in an airtight container for months.

Preparation time: About 5 minutes

Yield: About 1 cup

TOASTED CUMIN AND BLACK PEPPER RUB

The slightly smoky flavor of toasted cumin enhances the inherent wildness and woodsiness of any game meat. The combination of cumin and black pepper is wonderful and seems somehow mysterious, harkening back to more primitive times. The hearty flavor of this rub is reminiscent of the aromas that pervade the open-air markets of Central America. For freshest flavor, use whole cumin seeds and grind them yourself; store-bought ground cumin is more likely to be stale.

¼ **cup cumin seeds**
2 **tablespoons dried oregano**
I **tablespoon black peppercorns**
¼ **teaspoon salt**
½ **teaspoon sugar**

Place all the ingredients in a dry skillet and toast over medium heat for 2 minutes until fragrant. Transfer to a spice grinder and pulse until smooth.

Serving suggestions: Rub on meats before grilling. This is especially good on rack of lamb.

Storage: Keeps well in an airtight container for months.

Variation: Add a little dried chipotle chile powder to the rub to add smokiness and heat.

Preparation time: About 5 minutes

Yield: About ½ cup

HERB BUTTER RUB

You often see herbed bread crumb crusts on racks or roasts of lamb or pork, especially at Easter time. Creating breaded herb crusts probably goes back to the age-old tradition of baking poultry or fish in a dough casing; this technique for providing texture and preserving moisture and flavor is common to the cuisines of many countries. This is a straightforward recipe that will add flavoring to baked fish and give it a bit of a crust.

8 **ounces (I cup) unsalted butter, softened**
I **egg**
2 **tablespoons fresh fine bread crumbs**
½ **cup chopped fresh parsley leaves**
2 **tablespoons chopped fresh thyme leaves**

Combine all the ingredients in a mixing bowl. If not using immediately, keep refrigerated.

Serving suggestions: Spread over fish before baking. Can also be used on chicken or lamb.

Storage: Keeps refrigerated for up to 1 week.

Preparation time: About 10 minutes

Yield: About 1¾ cups

SPICY PIÑON MUSTARD CRUST

Pine nuts grow on the low, bushy piñon trees that dot the Southwestern landscape, especially in northern New Mexico. They are harvested in late fall, when it is common to see whole families harvesting pine nuts by shaking the piñon trees so that kernels rain down out of the pine cones onto sheets spread below. The kernels are then split open, yielding the pine nuts. Pine nuts (also known as piñons) are rich and have a resiny taste that goes well with wild Southwestern flavors. Historically, pine nuts were an important staple for Native Americans of the Southwest; the Pima tribe, for instance, had more than 200 culinary uses for them, including grinding them into flour. The pine nuts grown in the Southwest are a different variety from those that come from the Mediterranean or China. The latter are somewhat sweeter and contain more oil. As with herbs and spices, pine nuts must be toasted very carefully, as they burn easily; knowing that they are expensive will no doubt sharpen your concentration! In this recipe, the mustard acts as a perfect foil for the richness of the pine nuts.

2 cups vegetable oil
12 6-inch corn tortillas
$\frac{1}{2}$ cup pine nuts (piñons)
$\frac{1}{4}$ cup Dijon mustard
$\frac{1}{2}$ cup peanut oil
2 tablespoons honey
2 tablespoons pure red chile powder
1 tablespoon chopped fresh rosemary leaves
$\frac{1}{4}$ teaspoon salt

Heat the oil in a skillet until lightly smoking and fry the tortillas until crisp, about 30 seconds. Drain on paper towels and let cool. Break the tortillas into pieces and place in a food processor with the pine nuts. Pulse until coarsely ground but not smooth. Transfer to a bowl and mix thoroughly with the mustard, peanut oil, honey, chile powder, rosemary, and salt.

Serving suggestions: Spread on lamb chops after searing them. Use it as a crust on fried or grilled chicken, or grilled rabbit.

Storage: Keeps in an airtight container in the refrigerator for about 1 week.

Preparation time: About 15 minutes

Yield: About 2 cups

SWEET RED BELL PEPPER AND CILANTRO MARINADE

Many people don't care for the taste of cilantro, at least the first time they try it, but its aromatic quality makes foods more appetizing. In this recipe, it freshens up the marinade, and contributes subtle grassy tones rather than a pungent or soapy flavor that it can sometimes give when used fresh in large amounts. This is a good all-purpose marinade for broiling, barbecuing, or roasting that will add zest to the food. It can also be used as a marinade for ceviches.

1 red bell pepper, seeded and cut into $\frac{1}{4}$-inch dice
2 tablespoons chopped fresh cilantro leaves
2 serrano chiles, with seeds, minced
Zest and juice of 1 large lemon
Zest and juice of 1 lime
Zest and juice of 1 orange
$\frac{1}{2}$ cup peanut oil
$\frac{1}{2}$ teaspoon salt

Mix all the ingredients together in a large bowl.

Serving suggestions: Use it to marinate shrimp, fish such as salmon, pork, chicken, and duck. Don't rub any of this marinade off before cooking. If you are grilling the food, it is best to do it over low heat.

Storage: Best used within 1 or 2 days, after which the citrus fruit begins to lose its fresh flavor.

Preparation time: About 30 minutes

Yield: About 1$\frac{1}{2}$ cups

TANGY TANGERINE AND TEQUILA MARINADE

Tequila is a Mexican distilled spirit produced from the blue agave plant. Most tequila is produced in just the three states of Jalisco, Nayarit, and Michoacán. Although for sipping, nothing beats an aged tequila or tequila añejo, for cooking I prefer to use a good-quality silver tequila (tequila plata), which has a pure flavor and does not taste of the wood barrels used in the aging process. (The plata comes straight from the still.) My friend Lucinda Hutson has recently completed a definitive book all about tequila (Tequila!, Ten Speed Press) in which she explains how tequila is made, and how it can be used in cooking as well as in cocktails.

Tequila is a natural partner for citrus fruit, margaritas cocktails being a case in point, and this marinade another.

¼ cup sugar

½ cup unseasoned rice vinegar

I teaspoon chile caribe

Zest and juice of 8 tangerines

3 tablespoons (I jigger) premium tequila, such as El Tesoro or Sauza Hornitos

I tablespoon fresh lime juice

I tablespoon peanut oil

I tablespoon chopped fresh mint leaves

¼ teaspoon salt

In a saucepan, bring the sugar, vinegar, and chile caribe to a boil. Add the tangerine zest, remove from heat, and let cool. Add the tangerine juice, tequila, lime juice, peanut oil, mint, and salt.

Serving suggestions: Use to marinate pork chops or ribs. Only use it with fish if you are making a ceviche.

Storage: Best used the same day or the next day.

Variation: Other citrus fruit, such as orange and grapefruit, can be used instead of tangerines.

Preparation time: About 15 minutes

Yield: About 1½ cups

GIN AND JUNIPER RANGE MARINADE

Juniper berries grow on low trees similar to the piñon tree. They are found throughout the Southwest, and are likewise a typical part of the scenery in northern New Mexico. In the late spring and summer sunshine, the piney aroma of the junipers and piñons is particularly heady. Juniper berries have a dark blue tinge, and a pungent and astringent flavor. They are one of the principal flavoring ingredients in gin. By combining the two ingredients in this recipe, each serves to reinforce the other. Gin was first used by the Dutch as a medicine in the seventeenth century, and soon became the popular drink of eighteenth century England, where its addictive qualities led it to be nicknamed "Mother's ruin."

12 juniper berries

3 cups good Burgundy-style red wine

6 tablespoons (2 jiggers) gin

½ onion, peeled and cut into ¼-inch dice

I carrot, peeled and cut into ¼-inch dice

I stick celery, cut into ¼-inch dice

I tablespoon chopped fresh thyme leaves

I tablespoon chopped fresh rosemary leaves

3 cloves garlic, peeled and crushed

4 black peppercorns, cracked

2 dried bay leaves

Zest and juice of I lime

Crack the juniper berries with a mortar and pestle or roll with a flat, heavy pan. This releases more of their flavor. Mix all the ingredients together in a large bowl.

Serving suggestions: Use to marinate game meats such as venison, quail, squab, or duck at room temperature for a few hours, or overnight in the refrigerator.

Storage: Keeps in the refrigerator for weeks.

Preparation time: About 10 minutes

Yield: About 4 cups

PINEAPPLE, BASIL, AND ORANGE MARINADE

Many herbs suggest fruit flavors, or at least have taste characteristics that hint at fruit tones. Good examples are lemon thyme and red sage. Pineapple basil, which is available at most good nurseries, exudes the aroma of tropical pineapple, and its taste is remarkably like that of the fruit. The aromatic qualities of fresh herbs are one of their most important features, and they should not be cut up too long before use or their essential oils will evaporate and disappear.

½ pineapple, cut into ¼-inch dice
1 cup fresh orange juice (4 oranges)
¼ cup unseasoned rice vinegar
2 tablespoons chopped fresh pineapple basil leaves, or sweet basil
¼ cup virgin olive oil
1 serrano chile, seeded and minced
¼ teaspoon salt

Place all the ingredients in a food processor and purée.

Serving suggestions: Use it to marinate fish or chicken for 30 minutes before cooking. Toss it with raw shrimp in the shell and roast the shrimp at 350 degrees for 10 to 15 minutes.

Storage: Best used the same day or the next day.

Variation: Add 2 tablespoons fresh passion fruit juice for a more tropical marinade.

Preparation time: About 15 minutes

Yield: About 2 cups

SPICY LIME AND CILANTRO MARINADE

This recipe gives food an aromatic, spicy "green" flavor and an attractive sheen. The combination of sweet and sour are natural counterpoints that yield satisfying flavor tones, especially with delicate or even bland foods. The flavors of lime and cilantro go together well. Fish and poultry should not be marinated for too long, as the acid of the lime juice will break down the flesh and "cook" it too much.

2 tablespoons fresh lime juice
2 teaspoons peanut oil
1 tablespoon unseasoned rice vinegar
1 tablespoon chopped fresh cilantro leaves
1 serrano chile, seeded and minced
Pinch of granulated sugar

In a mixing bowl, thoroughly combine all the ingredients.

Serving suggestions: Use it to marinate fish or chicken, or brush it on while grilling shellfish. Can be used to make a ceviche.

Storage: Best used the same day.

Preparation time: About 10 minutes

Yield: About 1 cup

MANGO SCOTCH BONNET CARIBBEAN BARBECUE GLAZE

The Scotch bonnet chile is closely related to the habanero chile, so close that the two can be used interchangeably. Both have a scorching heat, and both have strong tropical fruit flavors, with subtle tones of mango, orange, banana, and pineapple. The two chiles are used primarily in salsas and sauces. I find that the red and deep yellow Scotch bonnet and habanero chiles have the best flavor. My friend Chris Schlesinger produces a line of great sauces based on the Scotch bonnet chile. It's called Inner Beauty, and is available nationwide. I particularly like the description on the label: "Use Inner Beauty to enhance dull and boring food. Keep away from pets, open flames, children, and bad advice. This is not a toy. This is serious. Stand up straight, sit right, and stop mumbling. Warning: hottest sauce in North America." Chris's restaurants in Cambridge, Massachusetts, The Blue Room and The East Coast Grill, are places to go for a good time and great picante food.

2 tablespoons peanut oil

4 ripe mangoes, peeled, pitted, and cut into ½-inch dice

1 white onion, peeled and cut into ¼-inch dice

1 carrot, peeled and cut into ¼-inch dice

2 fresh orange Scotch bonnet or habanero chiles, seeded and finely minced

½ cup champagne vinegar

½ cup ketchup

¼ cup sugar

Salt to taste

In a saucepan, heat the peanut oil and sauté the mangoes, onion, carrot, and Scotch bonnet or habanero chiles for 10 minutes over medium heat, or until the onions are soft and translucent. Deglaze the saucepan with the vinegar, and add the ketchup and sugar. Bring to a slow boil, reduce heat, and simmer for 35 to 45 minutes. Remove pan from heat and season with salt. Transfer to a food processor or blender, and pulse. Strain through a medium sieve; if the sauce is too thick, add a little water to thin.

Serving suggestions: Use as a barbecue sauce with grilled seafood such as lobster, crab, and scallops, and with pork. Can be brushed on as a glaze during cooking.

Storage: Holds well for weeks in the refrigerator.

Preparation time: About 1½ hours

Yield: About 3 cups

SPICY CHIPOTLE TOLTEC BARBECUE GLAZE

The Toltecs were a warring Nahuatl society that succeeded the Mayan civilization from Tula, in Central Mexico, and reached its peak between the ninth and eleventh centuries. Their influence can be seen at Chichén Itzá, *the spectacular archaeological site in the Yucatán. The Toltecs used skulls as one of their forbidding architectural motifs, especially for their altar platforms, befitting their fearsome reputation. This sauce is as ferocious as the Toltecs were themselves, and goes well with the slain beast barbecuing in your backyard. Make no mistake – this glaze is not for dainty tea parties!*

1 cup unseasoned rice vinegar

1 cup cider vinegar

2 tablespoons coriander seeds

1 tablespoon whole cloves

6 allspice berries

¼ cup virgin olive oil

1 medium onion, cut into ⅛-inch dice

4 cloves roasted garlic, peeled and minced

1 cup brown sugar

¼ cup molasses

1 tablespoon Worcestershire sauce

1 bottle dark beer, such as **Negra Modelo, Dos Equis,** or **Beck's**

½ cup chipotle chile purée (page 120)

1½ 14-ounce bottles ketchup

Put the rice and cider vinegars in a saucepan, add the coriander, cloves, and allspice, and bring to a boil. Reduce the liquid by half, strain, and set aside.

In a separate pan, heat the olive oil and sauté the onion over medium heat until slightly caramelized. Add the garlic and brown sugar, and cook until the sugar melts, about 1 minute. Add the molasses and Worcestershire sauce, and deglaze the pan with the beer.

Add the reserved vinegar mixture and chipotle chile purée to the pan, and simmer over low heat for 1 hour. Add the ketchup, and cook for a further 10 minutes. Strain the mixture, pushing down on the ingredients to extract all the juices.

Serving suggestions: Brush this barbecue glaze on chicken or ribs for delicious, smoky, hot results. We add a little of this glaze to black beans as the perfect finishing touch (page 110).

Storage: Keeps for up to 2 weeks in the refrigerator.

Preparation time: About 2½ hours

Yield: About 4 cups

OVEN-ROASTED GARLIC BARBECUE GLAZE

This is a glaze for garlic lovers – we know you're out there! The pungent flavor of garlic is seriously diminished by the roasting process, so this glaze will have the sweet taste of roasted garlic, but won't leave you with that embarrassing garlic breath! Garlic is in peak season from early to mid-summer. Buy garlic that is firm and full, heavy for its size, and without any green sprouting parts. If you can get it, use the purple-tinted variety of garlic.

½ **cup unseasoned rice vinegar**
½ **cup cider vinegar**
1 **tablespoon coriander seeds**
½ **tablespoon whole cloves**
3 **allspice berries**
2 **tablespoons virgin olive oil**
½ **white onion, cut into ½-inch dice**
1 **head roasted garlic, peeled and sliced**
¼ **cup brown sugar**
1 **tablespoon dark molasses**
½ **tablespoon Worcestershire sauce**
½ **bottle dark beer, such as Negra Modelo, Dos Equis, or Beck's**
1 **14-ounce bottle ketchup (1¾ cups)**
½ **tablespoon salt**

Place the rice and cider vinegars in a saucepan, add the coriander, cloves, and allspice, and bring to a boil. Reduce the liquid by half, strain, and set aside.

In a separate pan, heat the olive oil and sauté the onion and garlic for 5 minutes over medium heat. Lower the heat and stir in the sugar until it melts, about 1 minute. Add the molasses and Worcestershire sauce, and bring to a simmer, keeping the heat low so that the sugars in the glaze don't caramelize and burn. Deglaze the pan with the beer and reserved vinegar mixture.

Reduce heat to low and simmer for 30 minutes. Add the ketchup, and simmer for 15 minutes longer. Strain through a fine sieve, pushing down on the garlic to extract the juices.

Serving suggestions: Can be used both as a sauce (like ketchup) or as a glaze. Good with chicken, ribs, and burgers.

Storage: Holds well in the refrigerator for up to 2 weeks.

Preparation time: About 1 hour

Yield: About 4 cups

CASCABEL COFFEE BARBECUE GLAZE

Normally, Southwestern barbecue sauces contain picante *chiles, such as the cayenne, which contribute plenty of heat but little flavor. This sauce uses the dried cascabel chile, which is medium-hot but very flavorful, and provides a whole new dimension with its smoky, nutty, coffee tones. Cascabels are small reddish-brown round chiles. When they are shaken, their seeds rattle, and this is how they got their name (in Spanish* cascabel *means "rattle" or "jingle bell"). Coffee was a fairly common ingredient in old-fashioned barbecue sauces. The combination of coffee and cascabel chiles is a natural, as this glaze proves. Make sure the glaze is cooked over low heat to prevent the sugars from caramelizing and burning. The cascabel chile purée can be made up to 2 days ahead of time.*

1 tablespoon virgin olive oil

2 tablespoons white onion, cut into ¹/₂-inch dice

2 cloves roasted garlic, peeled and minced

¹/₂ cup brown sugar

¹/₂ tablespoon dark molasses

¹/₂ teaspoon ground whole cloves

¹/₂ teaspoon freshly ground nutmeg

3 allspice berries, ground

¹/₂ cup unseasoned rice vinegar

¹/₂ cup cider vinegar

1 cup cascabel chile purée (page 120)

1 cup ketchup

1 cup strong coffee

¹/₂ cup water

Salt to taste

¹/₄ cup espresso coffee (optional)

In a saucepan, heat the oil and sauté the onion and garlic for 5 minutes over medium heat. Stir in the sugar, molasses, cloves, nutmeg, and allspice. Deglaze with both the rice and cider vinegars and bring to a simmer. Add the cascabel chile purée and ketchup, and return to a low simmer. Add the coffee and water, return to a simmer, and cook for 20 minutes. For a stronger coffee flavor, add the espresso at the end.

Season with salt, transfer to a blender or food processor, and purée.

Serving suggestions: Use it as a barbecue sauce with grilled meats, especially pork. Also good as a dipping sauce for quesadillas and fries.

Storage: Keeps in the refrigerator for up to 1 week.

Preparation time: About 1 hour

Yield: About 4 cups

MEXICAN TAMARIND, RED CHILE, AND ORANGE GLAZE

Tamarind comes from Asia and Mexico, and is the fruit of an evergreen tree that was originally indigenous to West Africa. Tamarind pods contain some hard seeds and a bittersweet pulp that are boiled down to make a paste. Tamarind paste has a tart yet sweet flavor that naturally complements many food items, including chiles. It is a common ingredient in a variety of cuisines, and is also used as a flavoring in a number of food products (Worcestershire sauce and certain soft drinks, for instance). Tamarind paste is available in Latin, Indian, or oriental grocery stores.

4 ounces tamarind paste

4 cups water

$\frac{1}{2}$ cup honey

1 cup Mark's Red Chile Sauce (page 62), or Coyote's Red Chile Sauce (page 61)

Zest and juice of 4 oranges (about 6 tablespoons minced zest and 1 cup juice)

$\frac{1}{4}$ teaspoon salt

In a saucepan, break up the tamarind paste in the water. Bring to a low simmer and cook for 20 minutes, stirring occasionally. The mixture should have a liquid consistency; if it becomes too thick, add more water. Strain the mixture into a clean saucepan. Add the honey and red chile sauce, and bring to a simmer. Add the orange zest and juice, remove from heat, and let sit for 10 minutes. Season with salt.

Serving suggestions: Use it as a glaze when grilling chicken, quail, or pork, but make sure the fire is low to prevent the sugars from caramelizing and burning.

Storage: Keeps refrigerated for up to 1 week, but use as soon as possible to retain the fresh flavor of the orange juice.

Preparation time: About 45 minutes

Yield: About $2\frac{1}{2}$ cups

JEREZ SHERRY SHALLOT CIDER GLAZE

Although sherry is produced wherever grapes are grown, the finest sherries come from Jerez, a town in Andalusia, in southern Spain. It is made by the solera process, a complicated system of blending relatively new sherry with older sherries. There are numerous styles of sherry, each with its own flavor, sweetness, and color. For example, the creamier, darker amontillado *sherry has distinctive, sweet, nutty tones, while the light* fino *or* manzanilla *sherry has a delicate character and is very dry.*

Use the best quality fresh unfiltered cider available, and sherry vinegar which is sweeter than regular vinegar and has a more captivating aroma. Ideally of course, you would use a Spanish sherry and a Spanish sherry vinegar. It's especially important to have a fine sherry in the pantry, as it also makes a great apéritif.

2 cups fresh unfiltered apple cider

1 stick canela or cinnamon

2 whole cloves

2 allspice berries

15 shallots, minced and rinsed in cold water

$\frac{1}{2}$ cup Spanish sherry vinegar

1 tablespoon good-quality Spanish fino sherry

$\frac{1}{2}$ cup peanut oil

$\frac{1}{4}$ teaspoon salt

In a saucepan, bring the cider, canela or cinnamon, cloves, and allspice to a boil and reduce by half, about 5 minutes. Let cool. Mix in the shallots, sherry vinegar, and sherry, whisk in the oil, and season with salt.

Serving suggestions: Use at room temperature as a marinade and/or brush it on chicken, quail, or pork while grilling. Also makes a good dressing for salad greens.

Storage: Keeps well in the refrigerator for up to 1 week.

Preparation time: About 30 minutes

Yield: About 2 cups

BOURBON AND MAPLE GLAZE

Bourbon is made from fermented corn grain, and originated in Bourbon County, Kentucky in the second half of the eighteenth century. It has long been the preferred drink in the South, and remains a favorite in Western roadhouse bars. It's a pretty safe bet that the two things you're sure to find in any bar in the Southwest are plenty of country and western music, and a lot of bourbon. Maple sugar is processed by boiling down maple syrup; both the sugar and the syrup were used by the Native Americans of the eastern United States.

8 ounces maple sugar
½ cup water
2 cups fresh unfiltered apple cider
¼ teaspoon salt
3 tablespoons (1 jigger) bourbon

In a saucepan, dissolve the maple sugar in the water. Bring to a boil, add the cider, and return to a simmer. Reduce the liquid by half, until thickened (about 10 minutes). Season with salt and stir in the bourbon.

Serving suggestions: Brush it on poultry while grilling (it is good with quail). Avoid direct contact with flames to prevent the sugars from caramelizing and burning.

Storage: Keeps well refrigerated for up to 1 week; add a splash more bourbon if keeping for more than a day or two.

Preparation time: About 40 minutes

Yield: About 1½ cups

DIXON BOSQUE PLUM AND RED CHILE GLAZE

Bosque plums are small, red, and tart in flavor, and grow in the orchards of the upper Rio Grande Valley. Sylvia Varga, a descendant of the Spanish settlers who planted the orchards there centuries ago, still carries on the family fruit-growing tradition at her farm, La Carreta, in Dixon. She makes wonderful homemade organic plum jams as well as other conserves and fruit products. We make this glaze when her plums come into season each year. Though you might not think so, plums and fruity red chiles make a great combination. This glaze should be cooked at a low temperature – below 200 degrees – to prevent it from caramelizing and burning. You may find a candy thermometer helpful for this.

15 plums (about 1 pound), halved, pitted, and sliced
1 peach, halved, pitted, and sliced
1 tablespoon pure red chile powder
1 teaspoon ground dried chile de árbol
¼ cup honey
1 cup water
½ tablespoon fresh lemon juice

In a saucepan over medium-low heat, bring the plums, peach, chile powder, ground chile de árbol, and honey to a simmer, stirring often. Add the water and lemon juice and cook at a simmer until thickened, about 20 to 30 minutes. Do not bring to a boil. Transfer to a blender, and purée.

Serving suggestions: Use it as a barbecue sauce with pork, chicken, or tuna steaks, or brush it on during grilling. If you are using it as a glaze, avoid flare-ups as the sugars will caramelize and burn.

Storage: Keeps refrigerated for up to 2 weeks.

Preparation time: About 45 minutes

Yield: About 3 cups

KETCHUPS, MUSTARDS, AND TASTY TRAIL FIXIN'S

People in the Southwest have always shared a common sense of destiny and adventure. In terms of the cuisine, this translates into a bold and creative style of cooking, and a willingness to borrow from the culinary traditions of all the peoples who have ever settled there or in regions nearby.

Each group of settlers brought with them the distinctive flavors and tastes of their homelands. Those who came west in prairie schooners, for instance, brought with them a special selection of tasty, homemade, all-purpose condiments that could be used to enliven meats, beans – all kinds of foods, especially the blander ones. Great pride was taken in family renditions of these sides and condiments, and old family recipes were jealously guarded and handed down by the pioneers from one generation to the next.

Along with these family recipes, people also used household management books that contained collections of "receipts," and covered all kinds of other subjects as well; for example, how to arrange special occasions such as weddings and funerals; how to make soap and candles; and how to set up a home. The most famous of these manuals was Mrs. Beeton's Book of Household Management, which was published in England in 1861. Glancing through that and some similar volumes from the time, we find some surprisingly adventurous recipes. For example, among the ketchup recipes are mushroom ketchup, walnut ketchup, lemon ketchup, pontac (elderberry) ketchup, and even ox-liver ketchup. Even though we think of ourselves as having eclectic, sophisticated palates, these books usually contained more exciting foods than we find today on our supermarket shelves.

In Modern Cookery in All Its Branches by Eliza Acton, published in 1846, the following excerpt refers to mushroom ketchup: "This, with the essence of anchovies, walnut catsup, Harvey's sauce, cavice, lemon-pickle, Chili, cucumber, and eschalot vinegar, will be all that is commonly needed for family use, but there is at the present day an extensive choice of these stores on sale, some of which are excellent." One conclusion we might draw, with apologies to our English editor, is that the British palate was more interesting in those days than now.

With the development of commercial food products in the nineteenth century, these interesting condiments became much more standardized and exhibited less personality. Fortunately, we are coming full circle, and people are now demanding less homogenized, more flavorful sides and condiments, especially in Southwestern cuisine, which continues to be influenced by a diversity of rich ethnic culinary traditions.

The do-it-yourself recipes in this chapter are the perfect accompaniments for the kind of informal get-togethers we specialize in here—outdoor barbecues, picnics, and deck parties. Most hold well for weeks, and also make great gifts. Don't be afraid to create your own spreads and condiments by adapting the recipes in earlier chapters, too.

SOUTH-OF-THE-BORDER SMOKED CHILE KETCHUP

North of the wimp border you find plenty of prissy lowlanders with about as much backbone as their bland ketchup. South of this border, there is as much personality and character as you can shake a chipotle chile at. Actually, here in the Southwest, we try not to make fun of Easterners, Northerners, and all other outlanders; it's just too easy to do! Now that we have your attention, let's move on to the origins of ketchup: during the 1600s, European sailors discovered an exotic spicy fish sauce in the Far East called ket-siap *that was used with all kinds of food. They brought this sauce back to Europe, where it was adapted and quickly caught on, and from there its use spread to North America. This is our Southwestern version, and it's definitely not for wimps.*

1 tablespoon virgin olive oil

1 small onion, cut into ½-inch dice

2 teaspoons freshly ground cumin

1 tablespoon lightly toasted dried oregano

½ cup sugar

1 cup unseasoned rice vinegar

½ cup Coyote's Red Chile Sauce (page 61), or Mark's Red Chile Sauce (page 62)

¼ cup chipotle chiles en adobo

8 plum tomatoes (about 1 pound), roasted and halved

2 tablespoons chopped fresh cilantro leaves

1 tablespoon salt

In a pan, heat the olive oil until lightly smoking and sauté the onion over medium heat until translucent, about 3 to 5 minutes. Add the cumin, oregano, and sugar, and stir to combine. Deglaze the pan with the vinegar. Stir in the chile sauce, chipotles, tomatoes, cilantro, and salt. Reduce heat to low and cook slowly for 1 hour to thoroughly blend the flavors. Transfer to a food processor or blender, purée, and strain. Add a little water if necessary to thin to the desired consistency.

Serving suggestions: Good with hamburgers, hot dogs, and fries.

Storage: This recipe holds very well in the refrigerator for weeks, and can be used like any spicy ketchup.

Variation: For a very quick and easy alternative, purée ¼ cup of chipotle chiles en adobo with a bottle of ketchup.

Preparation time: About 2 hours

Yield: About 3 cups

SAVORY CINNAMON KETCHUP

Spicy, savory condiments such as this one appear in collections of recipes from the eighteenth and nineteenth centuries, and are descended from sauces used in the European Renaissance era. In those days, and in the decades that followed, spices such as cinnamon from the Far East, cloves from Africa and Zanzibar, and allspice and ginger from Jamaica were considered highly exotic, and using them was a sign of great affluence. This type of condiment was also popular with the early settlers and pioneers of North America.

1 tablespoon virgin olive oil

1 small onion, cut into ¹/₂-inch dice

¹/₂ cup sugar

2 tablespoons ground cinnamon

6 allspice berries, ground (about 1 teaspoon)

1 teaspoon ground whole cloves

2 cups unseasoned rice vinegar

12 plum tomatoes (about 1¹/₂ pounds), roasted and halved

1 cup apple cider

1 tablespoon salt

¹/₂ cup fresh orange juice

In a saucepan, heat the oil and sauté the onion over medium heat until translucent, about 3 to 5 minutes. Add the sugar, cinnamon, allspice, and cloves, and stir together. Deglaze the pan with the vinegar. Stir in the tomatoes, cider, and salt. Reduce heat to low and simmer for 45 minutes to blend the flavors. Transfer the mixture to a food processor or blender and purée. Stir in the orange juice, and add a little water if necessary to thin to the desired consistency.

Serving suggestions: Good with hearty dishes such as meat loaf. Also good with burgers, hot dogs, and fries.

Storage: Holds for weeks in the refrigerator.

Preparation time: About 2 hours

Yield: About 4 cups

RED CHILE HORSERADISH

Horseradish is a member of the mustard family. In its raw state, it is the most pungent of all the edible roots, but when cooked, its fiery oils dissipate. Horseradish is native to southeastern Europe, but it is now cultivated throughout Europe as well as in the United States. In fact, it grows so easily that it is regarded as a weed in some areas. In Greek and Roman times, horseradish was used as a medicinal plant, and it was only in seventeenth century England that it became popular as a condiment (roast beef with horseradish remains a British staple). Blended with the red chile sauce, the horseradish is transformed into a zippy Southwestern condiment.

1 tablespoon virgin olive oil

¹/₂ cup freshly grated horseradish

¹/₂ white onion, cut into ¹/₄-inch dice

1 tablespoon Spanish sherry vinegar

1 cup Coyote's Red Chile Sauce (page 61), or Mark's Red Chile Sauce (page 62)

Pinch of salt

In a saucepan, heat the oil and sauté the horseradish and onion over medium heat for 5 minutes. Add the vinegar, red chile sauce, and salt. Simmer for about 10 minutes until the horseradish is softened. Transfer to a blender and purée.

Serving suggestions: Serve it as a condiment with grilled steaks, sausages, and ham.

Storage: Holds well in the refrigerator for up to 1 week.

Preparation time: About 30 minutes

Yield: About 1¹/₂ cups

CHILE ROJO "TWISTER" MUSTARD

Mustard is one of the oldest and most widely used of all the condiments. Its use dates back to the ancient Chinese, Egyptian, Greek, and Roman civilizations; French Dijon mustard has been made since the thirteenth century. There are three main types of mustard seed: white seeds (which actually vary in color from white to yellow) are used in most English and American mustards; brown seeds are used in most French mustards; and black seeds are used in German mustards.

Mustard and chiles make a wonderfully pungent combination. While mustard (like horseradish) affects the sinuses and nasal passage more than the palate, chiles make themselves felt in the mouth and on the tongue. The pairing here therefore adds up to a double whammy, and the recipe is aptly named after the "twister," a mechanical bull that bucks as well as jerks from side to side to throw the rider off. This mustard'll throw your taste buds for a loop!

2 tablespoons pure red chile powder
2 tablespoons water
2 cups Dijon mustard
¹⁄₂ cup Mayonnaise (page 121)
¹⁄₂ cup Coyote's Red Chile Sauce (page 61), or Mark's Red Chile Sauce (page 62)
¹⁄₂ bunch scallions, white and green parts, minced
2 tablespoons fresh lime juice
¹⁄₄ teaspoon salt

Stir the chile powder with the water in a mixing bowl to remove any lumps. Add the mustard, mayonnaise, red chile sauce, scallions, lime juice, and salt, mix together thoroughly, and refrigerate.

Serving suggestions: At Coyote Cafe, we serve this mustard with lamb sausages. It also goes well with all grilled meats, especially pork or lamb. Great for spicing up hot dogs.

Storage: Holds well in the refrigerator for weeks.

Preparation time: About 15 minutes

Yield: About 3 cups

HOT MAPLE DILL MUSTARD

These days, you can buy all kinds of flavored mustards, including basil, celery, garlic, honey, nettle, orange, and raspberry mustard, to name a few I've seen recently. This one is both sweet and hot; it gives an interesting taste sensation as the sweetness hits the tongue first, and then almost immediately, the heat kicks in. Dill is a sweet herb with anise and licorice tones: it has enjoyed a long and illustrious history throughout eastern and northern Europe. I associate this mustard with gravlax, salmon that has been cured with dill (a Scandinavian tradition).

¹⁄₂ cup strong pure maple syrup
I cup Dijon mustard
2 tablespoons chopped fresh dill weed
Chile caribe (optional)

Thoroughly combine all the ingredients in a mixing bowl. For a spicier mustard, add some chile caribe, to taste.

Serving suggestions: Serve with salmon, cold lamb, roast pork sandwiches, cured meats, and sausages.

Storage: Holds well in the refrigerator for weeks.

Preparation time: About 5 minutes

Yield: About 1 cup

PICANTE OLIVE-CUMIN MASH

Olives have great personality and taste, and they absorb other flavors well. This olive-based recipe is a Southwestern version of the French tapenade, which is a paste made with crushed black olives, capers, anchovies, and olive oil. Unfortunately, most Americans have only been exposed to the canned pitted or stuffed olives that come in a vinegary brine and have a bland, tinny taste. Mediterranean olives, on the other hand, are usually kept intact and are packed in a brine with herbs, so they retain plenty of their character. When buying olives, bear in mind that the smaller ones tend to be more flavorful, and that ripened black olives are more intense than the more aromatic but less ripe green olives.

½ small eggplant, cut into ½-inch slices
2 tablespoons virgin olive oil
I teaspoon cumin seeds
½ teaspoon dried oregano
I teaspoon chile caribe
½ cup green Spanish or Sicilian olives, pitted
½ cup Kalamata or Greek black olives, pitted
4 cloves roasted garlic, peeled and finely minced
I teaspoon anchovy paste or 2 anchovy fillets
¼ cup red wine vinegar
I tablespoon chopped fresh basil leaves
¼ cup extra virgin olive oil

Brush the eggplant with the olive oil and roast (or broil) over medium heat for 15 minutes. Set aside. Place the cumin seeds, oregano, and chile caribe in a spice mill and grind together. Transfer to a blender or food processor, add the roasted eggplant, olives, garlic, and anchovy paste or fillets, and blend together. Add the vinegar and basil, and pulse briefly. With the machine running, gradually add the olive oil in a steady stream to form a thick paste.

Serving suggestions: Spread on bread or croûtons to be served with salads, or with tomato or roasted bell pepper soups.

Storage: Keeps in the refrigerator for weeks.

Preparation time: About 30 minutes

Yield: About 1½ cups

SOUTHWESTERN HARISSA

This is our Southwestern adaptation of harissa, a fiery North African chile sauce that is made with similar ingredients. When I was a student in Paris, I would make special trips to the Latin and Arab quarter on the Left Bank to eat cheap, filling, delicious meals in the North African restaurants there. The highlight of these forays would be the harissa, which brought the couscous, stews, and soups to life. When I travel to Paris these days, I like to retreat from the fancier two- and three-star restaurants to get a hit of that good old harissa.

10 dried New Mexico red chiles, seeded and rehydrated
I teaspoon cumin seeds
I teaspoon ground canela or ½ teaspoon ground cinnamon
I teaspoon coriander seeds
2 allspice berries
I teaspoon caraway seeds
4 cloves roasted garlic, peeled and minced
2 tablespoons extra virgin olive oil
¼ teaspoon salt

Rehydrate the chiles (page 120) and remove the seeds. Place the cumin, canela or cinnamon, coriander, allspice, and caraway in a dry skillet and toast for 2 minutes over medium heat until fragrant. Transfer to a spice mill and grind together. Place in a blender or food processor with the rehydrated chiles, garlic, olive oil, and salt, and pulse. Add just enough plain water to form a thick paste.

Serving suggestions: Add a little to rice and posole to add flavor and heat.

Storage: Keeps in the refrigerator for weeks.

Preparation time: About 30 minutes

Yield: About 1½ cups

GALLINA CANYON ARUGULA PIÑON PESTO

The Gallina Indians were contemporaries of the Anasazi Indians, or "ancient ones," who occupied large areas of the Southwest in pre-Columbian times. The Gallinas settled in northern New Mexico, in the canyon region that now bears their name. It is in this canyon that my friend Elizabeth Berry has her spectacular organic ranch, set beneath 500-foot red sandstone cliffs. Elizabeth grows most of the specialty produce for Coyote Cafe, including the wonderful arugula that we use for this recipe. Amazingly enough, Elizabeth manages to run her business in its secluded location without electricity or phone. Her operation is very impressive, and proves that sustainable agriculture is possible without the use of modern technology or chemicals.

1 packed cup fresh young arugula leaves
4 tablespoons toasted pine nuts (piñons)
¼ cup grated Parmesan cheese (about 2 ounces)
2 cloves roasted garlic, peeled and minced
1 teaspoon pure red chile powder
½ cup virgin olive oil

Place the arugula, pine nuts, Parmesan cheese, garlic, and chile powder in a blender or food processor and blend until smooth. With the machine running, gradually add the olive oil in a steady stream to form a thick paste.

Serving suggestions: Drizzle it on green salads, or on fresh sliced tomatoes or cooked vegetables. Use it as a pasta sauce with fettuccine or linguine.

Storage: Keeps in the refrigerator for up to 1 week. Can be frozen.

Preparation time: About 10 minutes

Yield: About 1½ cups

ALBAHACA PECAN PESTO

This recipe uses pecans rather than the pine nuts that are traditional in pestos, or walnuts, which are also sometimes used. Pecans were used extensively by Native Americans (the word pecan *is derived from the Algonquian name for it); while they are associated most with Southern states, New Mexico is also a major producer of high-quality pecans. Albahaca is Spanish for sweet basil.*

3 tablespoons toasted pecans (page 120), cooled
1 cup fresh basil leaves
¼ cup freshly grated Parmesan cheese (about 2 ounces)
3 cloves garlic, peeled
Juice of ½ lemon
½ cup virgin olive oil

In a food processor or blender, blend the pecans, basil, Parmesan, garlic, and lemon juice until perfectly smooth. With the machine running, gradually add the olive oil in a steady stream to form a thick paste.

Serving suggestions: Add a dab to soups (good with bean, minestrone, and squash blossom soups). Can also be used as a rub for chicken or meat before grilling. Serve it with linguine or fettuccine.

Storage: Holds well in the refrigerator for weeks, and freezes well.

Preparation time: About 10 minutes

Yield: About 1½ cups

SAN LUIS ANCHO PIPIÁN

San Luis, north of Mexico City, is famous for its an-cho chiles. In the huge food market in Mexico City, the Mercado Merced, dozens of chile vendors mark their heaps of chiles with the name of the region where they were grown. The San Luis anchos are among the most expensive, as they are the sweetest, most refined anchos of all.

Pipiáns are sauces made with ground nuts or seeds and various spices; they date back to pre-Co-lumbian days. I like to think of them as Southwestern pestos. This particular one is made with ancho chiles and pine nuts.

5 dried ancho chiles
5 dried New Mexico red chiles
I or 2 cloves garlic, peeled
¼ teaspoon ground dried oregano
¼ teaspoon cumin seeds, toasted and ground
1½ tablespoons virgin olive oil
¼ cup pine nuts (piñons), toasted
Pinch of salt

Rehydrate the chiles (page 120). (You can soak them together if they seem to be of the same soft-ness. If not, rehydrate them separately.) Seed the chiles, and purée and strain them. Place the chile purée in a blender, add the garlic, and blend together. Add the oregano, cumin, and olive oil, and blend again. Add the pine nuts and blend, but be careful not to overmix as you do not want a com-pletely smooth sauce. Season with salt.

Serving suggestions: Use it like a cocktail sauce with cold seafood. Add a dab to venison chile or on grilled pork or ribs. Makes a good dip for fries, too.

Storage: Holds well for weeks.

Preparation time: About 1 hour

Yield: About 2 cups

SUN-DRIED TOMATO CAMPFIRE SPREAD

This spread can be used to make garlic toast in much the same way as the Italian bruschetta. *Spread this Southwestern version on some crusty bread and grill it over the campfire. Sun-dried tomatoes used to be expensive and difficult to find, but they are now rela-tively commonplace, both in the dry form and packed in oil. Either way, they are very handy ingredients to keep in the Southwestern pantry; their intense flavor and chewy texture adds a richness to many different sauces, spreads, and dressings. You can use either kind in this recipe.*

8 ounces sun-dried tomatoes
4 ripe plum tomatoes (about 8 ounces)
½ packed cup fresh basil leaves
2 shallots, peeled and cut into ½-inch dice and rinsed
4 cloves roasted garlic, peeled and minced
½ cup Italian balsamic vinegar
½ cup virgin olive oil
2 tablespoons pure chile powder
I teaspoon salt
I tablespoon freshly ground black pepper

If you are using sun-dried tomatoes that are not packed in oil, rehydrate them in warm water or oil to cover for 15 minutes. Meanwhile, blacken the plum tomatoes over a grill or gas flame. The best consistency is obtained by running the tomatoes, basil, shallots, and garlic through a meat grinder, but a food processor or blender can also be used. If you use a food processor or blender, pulse the sun-dried tomatoes, basil, shallots, and garlic so that they are thoroughly mixed but not puréed. Stir in the balsamic vinegar, oil, chile powder, salt, and pepper.

Serving suggestions: Spread on grilled bread or pizzas. Add a little to egg salad or cold lamb sand-wiches.

Storage: Keeps refrigerated for 7 to 10 days.

Variation: This recipe can be adapted as a dressing by adding more oil and vinegar.

Preparation time: About 1 hour

Yield: About 2½ cups

CHIPOTLE MAYONNAISE

The origin of the French word mayonnaise, *to describe an emulsion of egg yolks, oil, lemon juice or vinegar, and seasonings, is disputed. In his excellent reference work,* The Dictionary of American Food and Drink, *John Mariani reviews a number of various theories: that the word should properly be* moyeunaise, *from the French* moyeu *(egg yolk);* magnonaise, *from* manier *(to stir); or that the word refers to a sauce created in the 1750s by the chef of the Duke of Richelieu to commemorate the successful siege and capture of Port Mahon, the capital of Minorca in the Mediterranean Balearic Islands. John Mariani further reports that the word* mayonnaise *first appeared in the English language in 1841. This recipe makes a spicy mayonnaise that represents a simple and perfect culinary combination of the Old World and the New.*

1 egg plus 1 egg yolk
1 tablespoon fresh lemon juice
¼ cup chipotle chile purée (page 120)
1 clove garlic, peeled
1½ cups peanut oil

Place the egg, egg yolk, lemon juice, chipotle purée, and garlic in a blender or food processor and purée until smooth. With the machine running, pour in the oil in a slow and steady stream until completely absorbed and thick. Keep chilled.

Serving suggestions: Use as a spread for just about any type of sandwich or as a dressing for spicier potato and pasta salads.

Storage: Keeps refrigerated for up to 1 week.

Variation: If available, use pasilla de Oaxaca chiles, which are a type of smoked chile from southern Mexico. Rehydrate and purée them as you would any other dried chile (page 120), and substitute ¼ cup puréed pasilla de Oaxaca for the ¼ cup chipotle purée.

Preparation time: About 10 minutes

Yield: About 2 cups

BLACKENED SERRANO MAYONNAISE

This mayonnaise uses roasted fresh chiles rather than dried chiles as in the previous recipe, giving it quite a different flavor and character, while matching the heat quotient. Roasting the chiles creates a smokiness, but take care not to burn them, which will result in an acrid flavor.

10 serrano chiles
1 egg plus 1 egg yolk
1 tablespoon fresh lime juice
1 tablespoon chopped fresh cilantro leaves
1½ teaspoons salt
2 cups peanut oil

In a dry cast-iron skillet, on a grill, or on a rack over a flame, blacken the serranos. Allow to cool completely (the serranos must be cold when puréed or the mayonnaise will break and separate). Transfer to a blender or food processor, add the egg, egg yolk, lime juice, cilantro, and salt, and purée until smooth. With the machine running, pour in the oil in a slow and steady stream until completely absorbed and thick. Keep chilled.

Serving suggestions: Great as a spread for any kind of sandwich or as a dressing for cole slaw.

Storage: Keeps refrigerated for up to 1 week.

Preparation time: About 15 minutes

Yield: About 2¼ cups

BOUNTIFUL BEANS AND RAINBOW RICES

I guess you could say I was born with a dried bean in my mouth. Actually, you could say that about anyone who hails from New England, as beans are such a big part of the New England culinary heritage. Baked beans were a part of our family tradition. My mother would slow-bake the beans with molasses, dry mustard, and salt pork, and she'd start them on Friday evening, so their tantalizing aroma would waft through the house as they cooked overnight. We'd feast on them on Saturday, along with ham and brown bread, and I would look forward to snacking on the leftover cold beans in the refrigerator the following week. Beans are still one of my favorite foods, and they happened to have been the first food I ever cooked for myself.

After I left New England, I didn't have much to do with beans again until I began cooking with Latin ingredients. At my first restaurant, Fourth Street Grill in Berkeley, one of our trademark dishes was a black bean soup. James Beard came in one day and enjoyed it so much, he wrote up the recipe in a syndicated article that appeared in The New York Times and more than 250 other newspapers. Beans became so popular that we began serving black beans as a side dish instead of french fries. Since then, I've used all types of beans cooked all kinds of ways in all kinds of dishes at my restaurants.

Beans are one of the oldest foods in existence, and date back thousands of years. There are three types of bean: the oriental soybean; the European broad bean (also known as the fava bean or horsebean); and the American bean, which is a New World plant. Many different types of the latter were discovered across North America by the early explorers of the New World, from Cuba to Florida, the Northeast, the Midwest, and the Southwest. They were an important staple of Mesoamerican cultures, and of the Native Americans of the Southwest, who usually grew them in the same fields as their corn.

Dried beans are an excellent source of nutrition. They are high in protein and essential minerals, and in addition, are a great medium for carrying flavors. I have never understood why beans are looked down on in the United States, and often treated as cheap, low-class food. Fortunately, beans are now back in vogue, and they have been elevated to grace elegant bone china in some of the finest restaurants in the country. They are no longer (pardon the pun) has-beans!

Dried beans are a must in a Southwestern pantry, and Coyote always keeps a variety in his. They will keep for up to a year if stored in sealed containers in a cool, dark place. Before use, they should be sorted through and any foreign objects (and especially small stones) removed. Beans normally require soaking in water for several hours and preferably overnight; this improves their texture and digestibility. Leave them in a cool spot while soaking them so they're not tempted to begin fermenting. Presoaked beans that are on the market do not require such preparation but usually lack the texture of regular beans. Adding a little baking soda to the cooking water helps soften the beans, but do not add salt until the end of the cooking process as it only prevents the beans from softening.

JUMPIN' JALAPEÑO BEANS

These beans are not related to the Mexican jumping beans that have grubs inside them that make them jump occasionally. On the other hand, these spicy beans could make your dinner guests jump up and down in similar fashion! When adding herbs to beans (in this case chives), cook for a brief period only or toss them in at the end, as overcooking is likely to result in a medicinal taste. Also, add the salt at the end of the cooking process; otherwise, the salt will toughen the skin of the beans and prevent them from cooking properly.

- 1 cup mixed dried beans, such as pintos, limas, flageolets, and black beans
- 1 tablespoon virgin olive oil
- ½ small onion, peeled and cut into ¼-inch dice
- ¼ small red bell pepper, seeded and cut into ¼-inch dice
- ½ poblano chile, seeded and cut into ¼-inch dice
- 1 jalapeño chile, with seeds, cut into ⅛-inch dice
- 1 cup vegetable stock or water
- ½ teaspoon salt
- 1 tablespoon chopped chives

Carefully sort through the beans and remove any foreign objects. Rinse in a sieve and soak overnight. Drain and rinse the beans, place in a medium-sized pot, and add enough water to cover the beans by at least 2 or 3 inches. Slowly bring to a simmer and cook at a low simmer until just tender, about 1½ to 2 hours. Add more water as necessary to keep the beans covered. When cooked, there should be about 2½ cups beans. Drain the beans.

Heat the olive oil in a large pan and sauté the onion, bell pepper, poblano, and jalapeño over medium heat for 3 to 5 minutes, until softened. Stir in the cooked beans, add the stock or water, and cook for 10 minutes, reducing the liquid somewhat. Season with salt and add the chives.

Serving suggestions: A great vegetarian side dish. Add oil and vinegar to make a tasty bean salad.

Storage: Keeps refrigerated for 2 or 3 days.

Variation: This is one recipe where you can use canned jalapeños. Use the juice, too, reducing the vegetable stock proportionately to equal 1 cup of liquid.

Preparation time: About 2 to 2½ hours

Yield: About 3 cups

BORRACHO BEANS

We call these beans borracho because they are cooked with beer (in Spanish, borracho mean "drunk"). I'm not sure whether the beer in this Mexican dish was originally added intentionally, or whether it was a substitute for unsafe water. Perhaps it was the accidental addition by a soused trail cook! Depending on your location and the whim of the cook, this recipe could also be known as cowboy or vaquero *beans. The alcohol in the beer cooks off, and you could just as well use alcohol-free beer; it's the taste that counts, which is why I prefer to use a dark beer. "Lite" beer is strictly forbidden. These beans should be soupy in consistency rather than thick or broken down.*

- 1 cup dried pinto beans
- 1 tablespoon lard or vegetable oil
- ¼ small onion, peeled and cut into ¼-inch dice
- 6 serrano chiles, with seeds, minced
- 8 plum tomatoes (about 1 pound), cut into ¼-inch dice
- ⅔ cup (½ bottle) beer
- ¼ teaspoon salt
- 2 tablespoons chopped fresh cilantro leaves

Carefully sort through the beans and remove any foreign objects. Rinse in a sieve and soak overnight. Drain and rinse the beans, place in a medium-sized pot, and add enough water to cover the beans by at least 2 or 3 inches. Slowly bring to a simmer and cook at a low simmer until just tender, about 1½ to 2 hours. Add more water as necessary to keep the beans covered. When cooked, there should be about 2½ cups beans. Drain the beans.

Heat the lard or oil in a large pan and sauté the onions and serranos over medium heat for 5 minutes, until softened but not browned. Stir in the tomatoes, cooked beans, beer, and salt. Bring to a boil, reduce the heat, and simmer 10 to 15 minutes until thickened but some liquid still remains. Stir in the cilantro just before serving.

Serving suggestions: Good for buffets, barbecues, and picnics, especially as a side dish with grilled foods. Use also with nachos. These beans reheat well.

Storage: Keeps refrigerated for 2 or 3 days.

Preparation time: About 2 to 2½ hours

Yield: About 3 cups

RANCHERO BEANS

The rustic, spicy Mexican ranchero (ranch-style) sauce is a cousin of the Italian marinara sauce. In Mexico, it is served with everything from eggs and tamales to meat, poultry, and seafood. In this dish, it is used to flavor the humble bean. A good ranchero sauce should contain plenty of chiles to wake up the taste buds, and plenty of tomatoes, too: there's nothing more disappointing than an insipid, limp, weak, and watery tomato-based sauce.

1 cup dried white, pinto, or anasazi beans

3 serrano chiles

12 ripe plum tomatoes (about 1½ pounds)

2 tablespoons virgin olive oil

½ onion, peeled and cut into ½-inch dice

3 poblano chiles, roasted, peeled, seeded, and cut into 1-inch strips (page 119)

1 teaspoon salt

1 cup vegetable stock or water

1 tablespoon chopped fresh cilantro leaves

Carefully sort through the beans and remove any foreign objects. Rinse in a sieve and soak overnight. Drain and rinse the beans, place in a large pot and add enough water to cover the beans by at least 2 or 3 inches. Slowly bring to a simmer and cook at a low simmer until just tender, about 1½ to 2 hours. Add more water as necessary to keep the beans covered. When cooked, there should be about 2½ cups beans. Drain the beans.

While the beans are cooking, blacken the serranos in a dry cast-iron skillet, on a grill, or on a rack over a flame. Set them aside, and blacken the tomatoes. When cool, mince the serranos and roughly chop the tomatoes.

Heat the olive oil in a large pan and sauté the onions and serranos over medium heat for 5 minutes, until softened. Stir in the blackened tomatoes, poblanos, cooked beans, salt, and stock or water, and bring to a low simmer. Cook for 10 minutes until thickened; add a little more liquid if necessary. Stir in the cilantro just before serving.

Serving suggestions: These beans can be used as a vegetarian burrito filling, and as a side for grilled meats, sausages, game birds, or poultry.

Storage: Keeps refrigerated for 2 or 3 days.

Preparation time: About 2½ to 3 hours

Yield: About 3½ cups

BAYOU CREOLE BEANS

Mardi Gras (Fat Tuesday) is celebrated in style in New Orleans every year, to mark the beginning of Lent. For those who give up meat for Lent, beans are an excellent source of protein: the most famous dish tailor-made for this period of abstinence is the classic Creole red beans and rice.

For this dish, we have borrowed heavily from Cajun and Creole cuisines. It doesn't have the rice, but it does have the red beans, in addition to andouille sausage (a special Cajun or Creole smoked pork sausage), and gumbo filé powder (a Creole seasoning made from ground sassafras leaves). Andouille sausages are generally available at specialty or gourmet butchers and delis. You can substitute chorizo for it, if you wish.

I cup dried kidney beans

2 tablespoons lard or vegetable oil

2 strips bacon, cut into ½-inch dice

½ cup crumbled andouille or chorizo sausage

2 cloves garlic, peeled and puréed

½ poblano chile, seeded, and cut into ¼-inch dice

2 tablespoons seeded red bell pepper, cut into ¼-inch dice

I stick celery, cut into ¼-inch dice

3 scallions, green and white parts, thinly sliced

2 tablespoons pure red chile powder

½ teaspoon gumbo filé powder

I tablespoon all-purpose flour

I tablespoon Tabasco sauce

½ tablespoon Worcestershire sauce

4 cups water

Carefully sort through the beans and remove any foreign objects. Rinse in a sieve and soak overnight. Drain and rinse the beans, place in a medium-sized pot and add enough water to cover the beans by at least 2 or 3 inches. Slowly bring to a simmer and cook at a low simmer until just tender, about 1½ to 2 hours. Add more water as necessary to keep the beans covered. When cooked, there should be about 2½ cups beans. Drain the beans.

Melt the lard or oil in a large pan and sauté the bacon over medium heat for 5 minutes. Add the crumbled sausage, garlic, poblano, bell pepper, celery, and scallions, and sauté for 5 minutes longer, stirring occasionally. Add the chile powder, gumbo filé, flour, Tabasco sauce, and Worcestershire sauce, and cook for a few minutes until slightly thickened. Stir in the cooked beans and then slowly add the water, stirring to avoid any lumps. Simmer for about 30 minutes until the mixture has thickened.

Serving suggestions: Makes a good side dish for chicken, sausage, or shrimp.

Storage: Keeps refrigerated for 2 or 3 days.

Preparation time: About 2½ to 3 hours

Yield: 4 cups

GREEN CHILE BEANS

The combination of white beans and green chile makes an attractive presentation. Adding some red bell pepper or sun-dried tomatoes will give the dish an even more striking and festive appearance. Beans and chiles were used together for centuries by successive Mesoamerican cultures, as well as by the Native Americans of the Southwest. The Hohokam Indians based in Arizona between the sixth and tenth centuries were the first great farmers of the region, and grew over 100 varieties of beans, chiles, corn, and squash.

I cup dried white beans

I tablespoon lard or vegetable oil

¼ onion, peeled and cut into ¼-inch dice

4 to 5 fresh green New Mexico chiles, seeded and cut into ¼-inch dice, or 4 ounces frozen diced green chiles

¼ teaspoon ground dried oregano

½ teaspoon salt

I cup water

Carefully sort through the beans and remove any foreign objects. Rinse in a sieve and soak overnight. Drain and rinse the beans, place in a large pot, and add enough water to cover the beans by at least 2 or 3 inches. Slowly bring to a simmer and cook at a low simmer until just tender, about 1½ to 2 hours. Add more water as necessary to keep the beans covered. When cooked, there should be about 2½ cups beans. Drain the beans.

Melt the lard or oil in a large pan and sauté the onion and green chiles over medium heat for 5 minutes. Stir in the oregano, salt, and cooked beans. Add the water and simmer for 5 to 10 minutes.

Serving suggestions: Serve as a side dish with grilled chicken or fish, or with enchiladas or tacos.

Storage: Keeps refrigerated for 2 or 3 days.

Preparation time: About 2 to 2½ hours

Yield: About 3 cups

BANDITO BLACK BEANS

Black beans, also known as turtle beans, are denser and meatier than any other bean, and take a little longer to cook. They stand up well to strong flavors, absorbing them better than lighter, creamier beans (pinto beans, for example). Black beans are standard fare in Caribbean and Central American countries such as Cuba, Guatemala (where I first tasted them), Honduras, El Salvador, and rural parts of southern Mexico, where they are served as a side dish with almost every meal.

I teaspoon cumin seeds, toasted and ground

I teaspoon coriander seeds, toasted and ground

I teaspoon dried oregano, toasted and ground

2 cups dried black beans, thoroughly washed

4 quarts water

I onion, peeled and minced

4 cloves roasted garlic, peeled and minced

2 jalapeño chiles, seeded and finely chopped

2 dried bay leaves

I cup tomato purée

I tablespoon salt

I cup Spicy Chipotle Toltec Barbecue Glaze (page 87)

Place all the ingredients except for the salt and barbecue glaze in a large stock pot or saucepan. Bring to a boil, then reduce the heat and simmer slowly for 2½ hours, or until the beans are tender, adding more water if necessary to keep the beans covered.

Add the salt and barbecue glaze and cook until the sauce thickens and almost all the liquid has evaporated (about 10 minutes).

Serving suggestions: Goes well with grilled meat, poultry, or game fowl. At Coyote Cafe, we serve it with our famous Pecan-Grilled Cowboy Steak.

Storage: Keeps refrigerated for 2 or 3 days.

Variation: This recipe can be adapted as a soup by adding water, puréeing half of the beans, and then folding them back in to the other ingredients.

Preparation time: About 3 hours

Yield: About 4 cups

CAMPFIRE BARBECUE BEANS

We would give you the original Western recipe for barbecued beans, but we've found that it requires too much patience to put the beans on a barbecue spit, and even harder to carve them! Plus, you need the special bean holders (a little like corn cob holders) which are hard to find anymore. Seriously though, barbecue and beans has to be one of the great culinary combinations of all time. The concept is about as old as cowboys and horses, as beans were a staple in the chuck wagon days, when the "cookie" was judged by the quality of his beans.

1 cup dried pinto beans
1 tablespoon virgin olive oil
4 strips bacon, cut into ¹/₂-inch dice
¹/₄ onion, peeled and cut into ¹/₄-inch dice
2 cloves garlic, peeled and puréed
1 tablespoon brown sugar
2 tablespoons dark molasses
¹/₂ bottle (²/₃ cup) dark beer
2 tablespoons puréed chipotle chiles en adobo
2 tablespoons tomato purée
1 cup water
¹/₂ teaspoon salt

Carefully sort through the beans and remove any foreign objects. Rinse in a sieve and soak overnight. Drain and rinse the beans, place in a large pot, and add enough water to cover the beans by at least 2 or 3 inches. Slowly bring to a simmer and cook at a low simmer until just tender, about 1¹/₂ to 2 hours. Add more water as necessary to keep the beans covered. When cooked, there should be about 2¹/₂ cups beans. Drain the beans.

Heat the olive oil in a large pan and sauté the bacon over medium heat for 5 minutes. Add the onion and garlic, and sauté for 2 to 3 minutes longer. Stir in the brown sugar and molasses until dissolved. Add the beer, chipotle and tomato purées, and the water. Stir to mix thoroughly, and add the cooked beans. Continue to cook for a few minutes until thickened. Season with the salt.

Serving suggestions: These beans go well with grilled meats and poultry. They're especially good with hot dogs and burgers.

Storage: Keeps refrigerated for 2 or 3 days.

Preparation time: About 2 to 2¹/₂ hours

Yield: About 3¹/₂ cups

Rice is a cereal grass that has been cultivated in Asia for thousands of years, and it has long been a vital staple for most of the peoples of that continent. Globally, rice is even more important than wheat as a food crop, and it has been estimated that up to 50 percent of the world's population rely on it for sustenance.

Rice was introduced to Europe during the early Middle Ages, probably by the Spanish Moors. It was taken to the New World first by the Spanish, who introduced it to Mexico and the Southwest, and later by the English, who brought it to the colonies on the East Coast. From there it found its way to the southern colonies, where it was grown widely, and where it remains popular to this day. The United States now exports more rice than any other country, even though it produces only 2 to 3 percent of the world crop, compared to the 90 percent grown in Asia.

Rice absorbs flavors well. One way to flavor rice is through the liquid used to cook it. For example, you can use a juicer or blender to liquidize different fruits or vegetables such as chiles, carrots, beets, or pears to zip up and enliven the rice. Another way is to fold in seasonings or diced fruit, nuts, or vegetables. And some recipes call for sautéing the rice with savory ingredients before adding the liquid. Flavored rice can be used as a side and it makes great stuffings for poultry.

I prefer to use an all-purpose rice such as Texmati for Southwestern dishes. Texmati is grown in Texas and California, and is a cross between American long-grain rice and the aromatic Basmati rice, which comes from India. It is a flavorful hybrid, and after it is cooked, the grains separate easily, giving it a pleasing texture.

Wild rice was an important part of the Native American diet, hence its alternative name of Indian rice. It is not in fact a rice, but a long-grain grass native to Minnesota and the Great Lakes region. Wild rice has to be carefully cleaned, but the effort is worth it as it has a delicious, nutty flavor that combines well with many Southwestern foods.

SWEET CINNAMON RICE

This dish is the ideal foil for hot and spicy food. There is no sugar in it, but the cinnamon suggests sweetness. It's a good example of an adaptable recipe to which you can add all kinds of dried or fresh herbs, fruit or vegetable juices, and nuts, as you wish.

2 cups white long-grain rice
4 tablespoons unsalted butter
2 small carrots, peeled and cut into $\frac{1}{8}$-inch dice
1 stick celery, cut into $\frac{1}{8}$-inch dice
1 white onion, peeled and cut into $\frac{1}{8}$-inch dice
$\frac{1}{2}$ teaspoon salt
4 sticks canela, or 1 tablespoon ground cinnamon
$\frac{1}{2}$ cup dried currants
6 cups water

Rinse the rice in cold water and drain. Melt 2 tablespoons of the butter in a large pan and sauté the carrots, celery, and onion over low heat for 10 minutes, stirring occasionally. Add the rice, salt, canela or cinnamon, currants, and water, and bring to a boil over high heat. When the water has reduced down to the level of the rice, reduce the heat to low, cover, and simmer for 15 to 20 minutes, stirring occasionally. Remove from heat and let stand for 5 minutes. Remove the canela, add the remaining 2 tablespoons of butter, and fluff up with a wooden spoon.

Serving suggestions: Serve with grilled chicken or quail, fish, or seafood. Also good with lamb or goat.

Storage: Keeps for 2 days in the refrigerator before it begins to lose its flavor.

Variations: Fold in some mint, marjoram, or basil at the end, or some toasted almonds, hazelnuts, pine nuts, or pecans. Substitute pineapple juice, apple cider or coconut milk for all or part of the water.

Preparation time: About 45 minutes

Yield: About 6 cups

CLASSIC GREEN RICE

This recipe is adapted from a version made by Diana Kennedy, the renowned author of several excellent books on Mexican cuisine. This green rice carries the pronounced flavors of the herbs very well, and you can add additional herbs and spices to your taste. The poblanos give the rice a satisfying, smoky quality, and the serranos make the dish hot and spicy. Take care not to overestimate the water, as no one enjoys gummy rice (except people without any teeth).

2 cups white long-grain rice
4 leaves romaine lettuce
6 poblano chiles, roasted, peeled, seeded, and roughly chopped
2 serrano chiles, roasted, peeled, and seeded
2 cloves garlic, peeled
$\frac{1}{4}$ white onion, peeled and minced
1 cup loosely packed fresh cilantro leaves
$\frac{1}{2}$ cup fresh parsley leaves
$3\frac{1}{2}$ cups water
5 tablespoons unsalted butter
2 teaspoons salt
$\frac{1}{4}$ cup chopped fresh cilantro or basil (optional)

Rinse the rice in cold water and drain. In a blender or food processor, purée the lettuce, chiles, garlic, onion, cilantro, parsley, and water. Melt 3 tablespoons of the butter in a large pan, add the rice, and cook over medium heat until translucent, stirring occasionally and taking care not to scorch the butter.

Add the puréed ingredients and the salt, bring to a boil, and cook for 2 minutes. Reduce the heat, cover, and simmer for 20 to 25 minutes until the water has just evaporated. Remove from heat and let stand for 5 minutes. Add the remaining 2 tablespoons butter and fluff up with a wooden spoon. Garnish with chopped cilantro or basil, if desired.

Serving suggestions: Serve with barbecued chicken, rabbit, fish, or seafood instead of the usual beans. Can be used with cheese and beans as a filling for burritos.

Storage: Keeps for 2 to 3 days in the refrigerator.

Variation: You can add orange zest, epazote, hoja santa (yerba santa), basil, or marjoram for different flavor accents. Purée them along with the lettuce and chives.

Preparation time: About 45 minutes

Yield: About 6 cups

PRAIRIE FIRE REDDENED RICE

The red-tinged, so-called Mexican or Spanish rice you see in most restaurants all too often is a tasteless, glutinous glob: a lost soul occupying the purgatory of side dishes and the hell of combination plates. This is too bad, because the real dish has plenty of personality and should take center stage in many Southwestern dishes. When we serve this rice at Coyote Cafe, our guests are pleasantly surprised by its character as soon as they take a forkful. This is a real trailblazer of a rice, and to achieve the best results, you must use a good, fresh chile powder.

2 cups white long-grain rice
4 tablespoons unsalted butter
2 cloves garlic, peeled and minced
1/2 onion, peeled and minced
4 1/2 cups water
1 teaspoon dried oregano, toasted and ground
1 teaspoon cumin seed, toasted and ground
1 tablespoon minced fresh marjoram leaves
1/3 cup medium-hot pure chile powder
1 teaspoon salt

Rinse the rice in cold water and drain. Melt the butter in a large pan or skillet and sauté the garlic and onion over medium heat for 6 to 8 minutes until soft. Add all the remaining ingredients, bring to a boil, and cook for 2 minutes. Reduce the heat, cover, and simmer for 20 to 25 minutes until the water has just evaporated. Remove from heat and let stand for 5 minutes. Fluff up with a wooden spoon, adding a little butter if desired. This rice can be kept warm and held for up to 2 hours.

Serving suggestions: Serve with grilled chicken, fish, or seafood. Also good with beef tacos.

Storage: Keeps for 2 to 3 days in the refrigerator.

Preparation time: About 45 minutes

Yield: About 6 cups

COWPOKE SMOKED RICE

The first time I made "smoked" rice, it was an unfortunate mistake. I had unknowingly burned the rice, and when I served it, my guests politely asked if I had smoked the rice. What made this episode even more embarrassing was that I was cooking for discerning (but diplomatic) Asian guests. A happier experience I had with smoked rice was a breakfast dish I once enjoyed at the fisherman's market in Rangoon, Burma. It consisted of flaming-hot stir-fried rice with shrimp and hearts of banana trees – quite a change of pace from Rice Krispies! What follows is a much simpler way to make "smoked" rice – by cooking it with chipotle chiles, which are smoked jalapeños.

2 cups white long-grain rice
4 cups water
12 ripe plum tomatoes (about 1 1/2 pounds)
1/4 cup puréed chipotle chiles en adobo
1/2 teaspoon salt

Rinse the rice in cold water and drain. Place the rice in a saucepan with the 4 cups water, bring to a boil, and stir with a wooden spoon. Reduce the heat, cover, and simmer for 15 to 20 minutes until the water has just evaporated. Remove from heat and let stand for 5 minutes.

Meanwhile, blacken the tomatoes on a rack over a gas burner, over a grill, or use a hand-held butane torch (available from hardware stores). Roughly chop the blackened tomatoes and fold into the rice, together with the chipotle purée and the salt.

Serving suggestions: Good with grilled meats and fish, or with vegetables as a tasty vegetarian meal.

Storage: Keeps for 2 to 3 days in the refrigerator.

Preparation time: About 30 minutes

Yield: About 6 cups

PINE NUT RICE

This is another fall rice that reflects the seasonal aromas of the high chaparral, when the yellow-flowered chamisa is in bloom, and the aroma of sage, piñon, and juniper fills the crisp, bright air. One interesting fact about the pine nut (piñon) crop is that there are never two consecutive years of bumper harvests; it's as though the trees rest up after a particularly plentiful year.

2 cups white long-grain rice
4 cups water
1 cup pine nuts (piñons), toasted (page 120)
¼ cup chopped fresh thyme leaves
½ tablespoon salt

Rinse the rice in cold water and drain. Place the rice in a saucepan with the water, bring to a boil, and stir with a wooden spoon. Reduce the heat, cover, and simmer for 15 to 20 minutes until the water has just evaporated. Remove from heat and let stand for 5 minutes.

Chop half of the nuts and mix together with the remaining whole nuts and the thyme and salt. Fold into the cooked rice just before serving.

Serving suggestion: The perfect accompaniment for delicately flavored fish such as sole, halibut, bass, turbot, or perch.

Storage: Keeps for 2 to 3 days in the refrigerator.

Preparation time: About 45 minutes

Yield: About 6 cups

TROPICAL TAMARIND COCONUT RICE

Rice dishes are an important element in the cuisines of the Caribbean. This recipe includes many of the tropical flavors I particularly like. It's a favorite of Coyote himself, who was sent the recipe by his tanned cousin who lives somewhere out on a coconut plantation in Barbados. For more information on tamarind paste, see page 90.

2 cups white long-grain rice
2 tablespoons unsalted butter
4 shallots, peeled and minced
1 teaspoon ground cinnamon
1 teaspoon ground allspice
2 ounces tamarind paste
2 cups water
1 cup fresh coconut milk
1½ tablespoons salt
¼ cup toasted coconut (page 120)
¼ cup toasted almonds (page 120)
¼ cup raisins or currants

Rinse the rice in cold water and drain. In a saucepan, melt the butter over low heat and briefly sauté the rice and shallots until the shallots become translucent. Stir in the cinnamon, allspice, and tamarind. Add the water, coconut milk, and salt, and bring to a boil. Reduce the heat, cover, and simmer for 10 to 15 minutes until the liquid is absorbed. Remove from heat and let stand for 5 minutes. Fold the coconut, almonds, and raisins into the cooked rice just before serving.

Serving suggestions: For a perfect tropical meal, serve this rice dish with grilled fish, poultry, pork, or ribs, accompanied by a fruit salsa.

Storage: Keeps for 2 to 3 days in the refrigerator.

Variation: Adding a little jerked chicken makes this recipe even more authentic: fold in ½ cup diced jerked chicken at the end.

Preparation time: About 45 minutes

Yield: About 6 cups

STONE FRUIT RICE

You can use any stone fruit for this Caribbean-influenced recipe – peaches, plums, nectarines, apricots, cherries, or even mangoes. It is colorful and keeps its consistency well because wild rice (also known as Indian rice) is firmer than regular long-grain rice. This dish is a natural for the early fall.

1 cup wild rice

1½ quarts water

2 tablespoons unsalted butter

½ onion, peeled and minced

¾ cup toasted chopped pecans (page 120)

3 tablespoons maple syrup

½ teaspoon salt

1 cup diced fresh stone fruit

Rinse the rice in cold water and drain. Place the rice in a saucepan with the 1½ quarts water, bring to a boil, and stir with a wooden spoon. Reduce the heat, cover, and simmer for 50 minutes to 1 hour, until the water has just evaporated. Remove from heat and let stand for 5 minutes.

Heat the butter in a pan and sauté the onion over medium heat for 2 minutes. Add the pecans, and stir. Add the maple syrup and salt and heat through. Fold into the cooked rice along with the diced fresh fruit.

Serving suggestions: A perfect fall dish, especially good with fowl. Also good with pork, game, and trout or salmon.

Storage: Best used immediately, but keeps for 2 to 3 days in the refrigerator.

Variation: Substitute ¾ cup dried cherries or cranberries for the fresh fruit. Rehydrate the dried fruit in warm water to cover. Drain, and sauté with the pecans.

Preparation time: About 1 to 1½ hours

Yield: About 6 cups

APPENDIX: BASIC TECHNIQUES AND RECIPES

ROASTING FRESH CHILES AND BELL PEPPERS

It is common to roast, peel, and seed fresh chiles and bell peppers when cooking with them. (Bell peppers are actually members of the chile family; when we speak of chiles in the directions that follow, that includes bell peppers, too.) Roasting chiles gives them a smoky tone and concentrates their natural sugars, intensifying their flavor. It also facilitates peeling off the tough skin. Most of the heat of chiles is contained in the seeds and internal ribs, so removing these parts will substantially reduce the heat.

Because they contain natural oils that can irritate or burn the skin, you should exercise caution when preparing chiles. Be careful not to touch your face or eyes, and be sure to wash your hands thoroughly when you are done. If your skin is very sensitive, wear rubber gloves, especially when you are working with the hotter chiles.

You can roast chiles on a grill, on a rack over an open gas flame, under a broiler, or with a hand-held butane torch. Turn them frequently until they blister and blacken all over, but do not burn the flesh. Transfer them to a bowl, cover with plastic wrap, and let them steam for 10 minutes until cool. Alternatively, the chiles may be placed in a brown paper bag; twist the top to secure. You can also cut the chiles in half and remove the seeds and membranes before roasting them.

When cool, peel off the skin with your fingers or with the tip of a knife. Do not wash the chiles under running water or the natural oils and flavor will be diluted. If you have not already done so, split the chiles open and remove the seeds and veins with a knife. Chiles may be roasted ahead of time and kept in the refrigerator for 2 to 3 days; they can also be frozen and stored.

REHYDRATING AND PURÉEING DRIED CHILES

It is common to rehydrate dried chiles before using them in Southwestern cuisine. They can then be puréed and added to sauces, soups, etc. You can purée chiles ahead of time; if you do not use them in a day or two, freeze them.

Stem and seed the chiles, and then dry-roast in a single layer in a large cast-iron skillet, or on a baking sheet in a 250-degree oven, for 2 to 3 minutes. Shake occasionally and do not allow to blacken or burn, or else the chiles will taste bitter.

Transfer the chiles to a large bowl and cover with enough hot or boiling water just to cover. Let stand for 20 to 30 minutes until they are rehydrated and soft. Transfer the chiles to a blender. Taste the water in which they were soaking, and if it is not bitter, add enough to the blender to make puréeing possible. If the water does taste bitter, use a little plain water. Purée the chiles and strain.

DRY-ROASTING GARLIC

Roasted garlic has a sweeter, more subtle flavor than fresh garlic. Fresh garlic should be roasted unpeeled, broken up into individual cloves. Place in a dry cast-iron skillet and roast over low heat for 30 to 40 minutes; shake occasionally to prevent the garlic from burning or roasting unevenly. Garlic can also be roasted in the oven: place the cloves in a 350-degree oven for 20 to 30 minutes or until lightly browned, shaking them occasionally. When the garlic is roasted, it should be creamy and sweet, and soft enough to squeeze out of the clove. Garlic can be roasted ahead of time.

DRY-ROASTING CORN

Cut the corn kernels from the cob, taking care not to cut too deeply into the tough cob. Place in a hot, dry skillet and roast in a single layer over medium-high heat for 10 minutes, shaking frequently.

ROASTING TOMATOES

Roasting tomatoes concentrates their flavor and dries out the excess moisture. To roast tomatoes, cut off the stems, cut the tomatoes in half lengthwise, and place on a wire rack or baking sheet, cut-side up. Roast in a 300-degree oven for 1½ hours, or longer, if necessary.

TOASTING HERBS, SPICES, SEEDS, AND NUTS

To toast herbs and spices such as oregano or cumin, place in a dry skillet over low heat and toast for 1 minute until fragrant, stirring frequently. Care should always be taken in toasting herbs and spices, as they must not be scorched, or they will taste bitter. It is best to toast each herb or spice separately, as they have variable toasting times and some burn more easily than others.

For seeds, toast in a dry skillet over medium-high heat for 2 to 3 minutes, stirring occasionally.

For nuts such as pecans or almonds, and for coconut meat, place in a single layer on a baking sheet and toast in a 300-degree oven for 10 to 15 minutes, or until lightly browned, stirring occasionally. Pine nuts burn very easily and should be watched carefully.

CRÈME FRAÎCHE

This is a tangy cream with a rich, thick texture. In France, it is made with unpasteurized cream, which gives it a richer flavor. In the United States, where cream is pasteurized, buttermilk or sour cream must be added to provide the necessary culture for the natural fermenting and thickening process to take place.

1 cup heavy cream
1 cup buttermilk or sour cream

In a stainless steel or other nonreactive saucepan, warm the cream to about 95 degrees (body temperature) over low heat. Do not overheat. Stir in the buttermilk, transfer to a clean glass or ceramic container, and cover tightly. Let sit in a warm place (70 to 80 degrees) for 24 hours. Stir, and then store in the refrigerator.

Storage: Keeps for at least 1 week in the refrigerator.

Yield: About 2 cups

MAYONNAISE

Homemade mayonnaise tastes so much better than store-bought that it's worth it to make your own. If you freeze the egg yolks and then bring them to room temperature, they will absorb more oil. For notes on the origin of the word mayonnaise, *see page 101.*

3 egg yolks
2 teaspoons Dijon mustard
1 tablespoon sherry or cider vinegar, or fresh lemon juice
1 teaspoon salt
2¼ teaspoons cayenne chile powder or pure red chile powder
2 cups peanut, canola, or safflower oil

Whisk together the egg yolks, mustard, vinegar or lemon juice, salt, and cayenne or chile powder in a mixing bowl. Gradually add the oil in a slow and steady stream, whisking continuously, until thoroughly incorporated. Taste, and adjust the seasoning if necessary. If you prefer, you can use a food processor to make the mayonnaise, but be sure to fit it with a plastic blade.

Storage: Keeps for up to 1 week in the refrigerator.

Yield: About 2¼ cups

SOURCE LIST

Coyote Cafe General Store
132 West Water Street
Santa Fe, NM 87501
Tel: (505) 982-2454

Chiles (including canned chipotles en adobo),
spices, herbs, canela, beans, nuts, tamarind,
Ibarra chocolate, masa harina, dried cherries
and cranberries, and other Southwestern
ingredients.

Los Chileros
PO Box 6215
Santa Fe, NM 87501
Tel: (505) 471-6967

Chiles.

Bueno Foods
2001 4th Street SW
Albuquerque, NM 87102
Tel: (505) 243-2722

Chiles, tortillas, masa harina.

Elizabeth Berry
Gallina Canyon Ranch
144 Camino Escondido
Santa Fe, NM 87501
Tel: (505) 982-4149

Beans and specialty produce.

Dean and Deluca
560 Broadway
New York, NY 10012
Tel: (212) 431-1691

Chiles, oils, vinegars, beans.

Monterrey Foods
3939 Brooklyn
Los Angeles, CA 90063
Tel: (213) 263-2143

Southwestern and Mexican products,
including chiles, canned chipotles, tamarind,
canela.

B. Riley
607A Juan Tabo Boulevard NE
Albuquerque, NM 87123
Tel: (505) 275-0902

Herbs (including epazote and hoja santa),
fresh mushrooms, greens, nopal cactus.

Italco Food Products
1340 S. Cherokee Street
Denver, CO 80223
Tel: (303) 722-1882

Spices, oils, vinegars, bacon, jerky.

Pacific Gourmet
PO Box 2071
San Rafael, CA 94912
Tel: (415) 641-8400

Oils, vinegars, spices, dried mushrooms, olives,
chocolate.

Bountiful Cow
Box B
1521 Center Street
Santa Fe, NM 87504
Tel: (505) 473-7911

Goat cheese.

Mozzarella Company
2944 Elm Street
Dallas, TX 75226
Tel: (800) 798-2954

Goat cheese, mozzarella, queso fresco, and
other cheeses.

Vea North America
1105 Greenfield
Waukegan, IL 60085
Tel: (708) 336-8443

Olive oil, olives, capers.

American Spoon Foods
411 E. Lake Street
Petoskey, MI 49770
Tel: (616) 347-9030

Dried cherries.

Del Valley Pecans
PO Box 104
Mesilla Park, NM 88047
Tel: (505) 524-1867

Pecans.

INDEX